CW00363037

Baedeker's
PRAGUE

Imprint

Cover picture: Hradčany Castle and Charles Bridge

78 colour photographs, 10 ground-plans, 4 special plans, 1 drawing, 1 transport plan (Metro), 1 city plan

Conception:
Redaktionsbüro Harenberg, Schwerte

Text:
Dr František Kafka

Editorial work and continuation:
Baedeker Stuttgart

English language:
Alec Court

General direction:
Dr Peter Baumgarten, Baedeker Stuttgart

Cartography:
Ingenieurbüro für Kartographie Huber & Oberländer, Munich

English translation:
James Hogarth

Source of illustrations:
Doležal (1), dpa (12), Historia-Photo (12), Jürgens (1), Kusak (13), Sperber (1), Stoll (37), ZEFA (1)

Following the tradition established by Karl Baedeker in 1844, sights of particular interest are distinguished by either one or two asterisks.

To make it easier to locate the various sights listed in the "A to Z" section of the Guide, their coordinates on the large city plan (and on the smaller inset plan of the city centre) are shown in red at the head of each entry.

Only a selection of hotels and restaurants can be given: no reflection is implied, therefore, on establishments not included.

In a time of rapid change it is difficult to ensure that all the information given is entirely accurate and up to date, and the possibility of error can never be entirely eliminated. Although the publishers can accept no responsibility for inaccuracies and omissions, they are always grateful for corrections and suggestions for improvement.

© Baedeker Stuttgart
Original German edition

© 1987 Jarrold and Sons Ltd
English language edition world-wide

© 1987 The Automobile Association 57480
United Kingdom and Ireland

US and Canadian Edition
Prentice Hall Press

Licensed user:
Mairs Geographischer Verlag GmbH & Co., Ostfildern-Kemnat bei Stuttgart

Reproductions:
Gölz Repro-Service GmbH, Ludwigsburg

Printed in Great Britain by Jarrold & Sons Ltd, Norwich

0-13-058215-8 US and Canada
0 86145 415 4 UK
3-87504-115-1 Germany

Contents

Preface

This Pocket Guide to Prague is one of the new generation of Baedeker guides.

Baedeker pocket guides, illustrated throughout in colour, are designed to meet the needs of the modern traveller. They are quick and easy to consult, with the principal features of interest described in alphabetical order and practical details about location, opening times, etc., shown in the margin.

Each city guide is divided into three parts. The first part gives a general account of the city, its history, notable personalities and so on; in the second part the principal sights are described; and the third part contains a variety of practical information designed to help visitors to find their way about and make the most of their stay.

The Baedeker pocket guides are noted for their concentration on essentials and their convenience of use. They contain numerous specially drawn plans and coloured illustrations. At the back of the book is a large plan of the city. Each entry in the main part of the guide gives the coordinates of the square on the plan in which the particular feature can be located. Users of this guide, therefore, will have no difficulty in finding what they want to see.

Facts and Figures

Prague's
coat of arms

General

Czechoslovakia – officially the Czechoslovak Socialist Republic – is a federal union of two States, the Czech Socialist Republic (capital Prague) and the Slovak Socialist Republic (capital Bratislava).

State

The country's official languages are Czech and Slovak, which have equal status.

Official languages

Prague (in Czech Praha), the "hundred-towered" or "golden" city on the Vltava (Moldau), is capital of the Czechoslovak Socialist Republic (ČSSR) and of the federal Czech Socialist Republic (ČSR), and is also the seat of the administration of the Prague city district and the region of Central Bohemia.

Capital

Prague lies in latitude 50° 05′ N and longitude 14° 25′ E in a basin in the Vltava Valley. It has an average altitude at river-level of 180 m (591 ft), rising to 383 m (1257 ft) in the White Mountain.

Geographical situation

From the United Kingdom: 010 42 2
From the United States or Canada: 011 42 2
To the United Kingdom: 00 44
To the United States or Canada: 00 1

Telephone dialling codes

In 1883 the old town of Prague had an area of 8·5 sq. km (3·3 sq. miles) and a population of 160,000. By 1901, after absorbing the neighbouring communes of Vyšehrad, Holešovice-Bubny and Libeň, it had increased in size to 21 sq. km (8·1 sq. miles), with a population of 216,000. In 1922 the local government entity of Greater Prague was established through the incorporation of 37 other districts, giving the city an area of 171 sq. km (66 sq. miles) and a population of 677,000. Prague now occupies an area of 497 sq. km (192 sq. miles) and has a population of about 1,180,000.

Area and population

Prague is divided for administrative purposes into ten wards. The first ward corresponds to the historic core of the city, taking in the Josefov quarter (the old Jewish quarter) and part of the Old Town (Staré Město), the New Town (Nové Město), the Malá Strana or Lesser Quarter and the Hradčany district.

City wards

The local government authority is the Central National Committee of 100 directly elected members, presided over by a *primator* (chairman). The ten wards have similarly constituted district committees.

Administration

◄ *Hradčany Castle and the Charles Bridge*

Population and Religion

Population

In the 14th c., during the reign of Charles IV, Prague was one of the largest cities in Europe, with a population of some 60,000. The blood-letting of the Thirty Years War led to a sharp decline in population, and by the end of the 17th c. Prague had no more than 40,000 inhabitants. The population began to increase again during the 18th and 19th c. with the establishment of the city's metropolitan function, and further impetus was given by the industrial development of the later 19th c. At the turn of the century the population passed the 200,000 mark. Thereafter the city continued to grow at a rapid pace, which was still further intensified by the incorporation of adjoining communes. By 1930 Prague had 849,000 inhabitants. The upward trend was maintained after the Second World War, and in 1960 the population reached a million. Since the mid 1960s the demographic curve has visibly flattened, and recent years have seen only hesitant progress towards the 1·2 million mark.

Ethnic composition

Prague's largest population group has traditionally consisted of the descendants of the original Slav peoples, in particular the Czechs. In the 14th c., the period of Prague's rapid development, there was a substantial German minority; but by the 19th c. this had shrunk to something of the order of 5 per cent. Over the centuries a considerable part in the city's life was played by the Jews, so that Prague came to be known as the "Jerusalem of Europe".

Religion

The majority religious belief in Prague has traditionally been Roman Catholicism. Second place is taken by the Czechoslovak Church (founded after 1918), which is Hussite. The largest Protestant community is the Slovak Evangelical Church of the Augsburg Confession. Recent estimates put the number of Jews at about 5000.

Transport

Port

The river harbour at Holešovice handles freight traffic, but is of no great commercial importance.
The Vltava is not navigable upstream from Prague, and even downstream is suitable only for vessels of modest size.
The landing-stage for passenger ships is on Engels Embankment (Nábřeží B. Engelse), near the Palacký Bridge.

Airport

Prague has a modern airport at Ruzyně, 20 km (12½ miles) north-west of the city centre. From Ruzyně the Czechoslovak national airline, ČSA, flies scheduled services to more than 50 cities throughout the world, and the airport is used by 24 international airlines.

Rail services

Prague is linked with the European railway network, and its Central Station (Hlavní nádraží) is the terminus for numerous national and international services.
Other stations handle traffic within Czechoslovakia and to the Eastern European countries. There are also almost 30 small suburban stations for passenger traffic.

Prague's Underground system (Metro) is still in course of development. So far 27 km (17 miles) have been brought into operation, and a further 10 km (6¼ miles) are due to be completed by 1990.

The trams are Prague's principal form of public transport, with services running on average at 15 minute intervals. Buses are mainly used to provide links with Underground stations and to serve outlying suburbs.

Important main roads (federal highways, European highways):

3 (E 14)	To Benešov, Votice, Tábor, České Budějovice and Linz
4	To Strakonice and Passau
5	To Plzeň (Pilsen) and Nuremberg (E 12)
6	To Nové Strašecí, Revničov and Karlovy Vary (Karlsbad)
7	To Slaný and Chomutov
8 (E 15)	To Lovosice, Teplice and Dresden
9	To Mělnik, Děčín and Dresden
10 (E 14)	To Mladá Boleslav, Turnov and Jelena Gora
11 (E 12)	To Poděbrady, Hradec Králové and Wroclaw
12	To Kolín
12 (E 15)	To Brno

Culture

Prague has been for centuries one of the great cultural centres of Europe. Since the foundation in 1348 of the Charles University, the first university in Central Europe, contributions to the intellectual history of the West in the fields of learning, literature and art have been made here. In our own day Prague is the cultural centre of Czechoslovakia, with 10 higher educational establishments, 26 adult art colleges, 34 technical schools, 226 general schools and 416 kindergartens.
Prague has 20 permanent theatres, including two opera-houses, three philharmonic orchestras and numbers of smaller musical ensembles.
Under the arrangements for the protection of ancient monuments over 2000 buildings, including many old churches, have been preserved from decay or destruction.

The Czechoslovak Academy of Sciences runs a considerable number of scientific institutes and research centres in Prague. The city also has an Academy of Art and a Conservatoire of Music.

Prague has several large libraries, more than 20 museums and numerous cultural organisations. Among the most important libraries are the National Library, the Municipal Public Library, the library of the National Museum and the National Medical Library.

Commerce and Industry

Industry

Prague is the economic centre of Czechoslovakia, and all the important national economic organisations have their head-quarters here. There are over 90 major industrial concerns in Prague, contributing almost 10 per cent of the total output of industrial products. A key position has traditionally been occupied by the engineering industry; and other important branches of industry, in addition to metallurgy and metal-processing, are pharmaceuticals, foodstuffs, papermaking and textiles.

Commerce

Long an important point of intersection of trade routes and the starting-point of the river-borne trade on the Vltava and the Elbe, Prague is still one of the leading commercial centres of Eastern Central Europe, and in recent years it has consolidated its reputation as a shopping centre, with more than a dozen large department stores and well over 4000 smaller shops offering a wide range of goods.

Tourism

Prague is one of the most popular tourist cities in Eastern Europe, and according to the latest estimates more than a million visitors come to the "golden city" from the western neighbour countries every year.

Notable Personalities

The Danish astronomer Tycho Brahe, already famous when he came to Prague in 1597, became Court Astronomer to the Emperor Rudolf II in 1599. He had previously built an observatory in Denmark, and his astronomical instruments were the largest of their day (the telescope not having yet been invented).

His observations provided the empirical basis for Kepler's laws of planetary movement, but he himself always remained an opponent of the heliocentric picture of the Universe. The Tychonian system, retaining the earth as the centre of the Universe, long continued to compete with the Copernican system.

Brahe's memorial slab, with his portrait, is in the Týn Church (see A to Z).

Peter Johann Brandl (or Brandel or Prantl), one of the great masters of Baroque art in Bohemia, was Court Artist to successive rulers of Bohemia and was also frequently employed by religious houses.

Subject to both Venetian and Flemish influences, he achieved a style of formal independence, based on his own vision and sensibility and showing marked realism. There are pictures by Brandl in a number of Prague churches.

Max Brod made his name mainly as the editor of Franz Kafka's writings, which – against Kafka's express wishes – he published posthumously. He himself was an Expressionist writer, with works such as "Tycho Brahes Weg zu Gott" ("The Redemption of Tycho Brahe"), "Über die Schönheit hässlicher Bilder" ("On the Beauty of Ugly Pictures"), "Streitbares Leben" (an autobiography) and "Die verkaufte Braut" ("The Bartered Bride"). He worked on the editorial staff of the "Prager Tagblatt" and was a member of the Prague Group. He wrote biographies of Kafka and the composer Janáček. In 1939 he emigrated to Tel Aviv.

After coming to Prague Christoph Dientzenhofer, one of a number of architects in this Bavarian family, worked nowhere else. Together with his talented son Kilian Ignaz he created the characteristic "Dientzenhofer Baroque", a synthesis of the old Bavarian system of pilasters and the baldacchino principle of the Italian architect Guarino Guarini, thus providing the basis for the last and finest phase of Central European Baroque church architecture. Buildings begun by the father in a somewhat conventional style were frequently carried to completion and stylistic perfection by the son.

Examples of this are Břevnov Abbey, the Church of the Nativity in Loreto and above all St Nicholas's Church in the Lesser Quarter, one of the most important churches of the Late Baroque period in Central Europe.

Among other buildings by Kilian Ignaz Dientzenhofer, now essential features not only of the townscape of Prague but of the whole Baroque cultural landscape of Bohemia, are the Villa Amerika and the churches of St John of Nepomuk on the Rock, St John of Nepomuk in the Hradčany and St Thomas. He also designed the Sylva-Taroucca Palace and the Kinsky Palace.

Tycho Brahe
Danish astronomer
(1546–1601)

Peter Johann Brandl
Bohemian painter
(1668–1735)

Max Brod
Prague writer
(1884–1968)

Christoph Dientzenhofer
(1655–1722)
Kilian Ignaz Dientzenhofer
(1689–1751)
German architects

Notable Personalities

Tycho Brahe

Antonin Dvořák

Albert Einstein

Antonín Dvořák
Czech composer
(1841–1904)

With his numerous chamber works and his great symphonies Dvořák paved the way for the emergence of distinctively Slav music. During his three years in America as Director of the National Conservatory in New York (1892–95) he also influenced many young American composers. This period is reflected in his most famous symphony, "From the New World".
Dvořák also achieved reputation as a composer of operas ("Rusalka", "The Jacobins").

Albert Einstein
German-American physicist
(1879–1955)

Albert Einstein, creator of the theory of relativity and the theory of gravitation, who received the Nobel Prize in 1921 for his contributions to quantum theory, was Professor of Theoretical Physics at the German University in Prague in 1911–12. There are commemorative plaques both on the building where he taught in the New Town (Viničná 1597/7) and on the house in which he lived in Prague-Smíchov (Lesnická 1215/7).

Václav (Wenceslas) Hollar
Bohemian etcher and draughtsman
(1607–77)

Václav or Wenceslas Hollar made his name with his etchings of Prague, London and various German towns. As a Protestant he was compelled to leave Bohemia in 1627, worked in Frankfurt as a pupil of Matthäus Merian and later in Strasburg and Cologne, travelled in Europe and North Africa and went to Britain, where he worked at the Court of Charles I. He died in London.
Hollar produced more than 3000 etchings and engravings. There is a large collection of his work in the Graphic Collection of the National Gallery in the Kinsky Palace (see A to Z).

Jan Hus
Czech reformer
(*c.* 1370–1415)

Jan Hus, Rector of the Charles University, preached in the Bethlehem Chapel against the authority of the Pope, criticised the secular possessions of the Church and called for a Bohemian national church. He was supported by the people and by King Wenceslas. In his "De ecclesia" ("On the Church") he set out his view of the Church as a non-hierarchical assembly of the faithful which acknowledged only Christ as its head, not the Pope. On the strength of a guarantee of protection by the German King Sigismund he appeared before the Council of Constance in 1415, accused of heresy. Refusing to retract his views, he was burned at the stake.
Hus's ideas formed the basis of the Bohemian Reformation, and

Jan Hus

Karl IV

Johannes Kepler

his death set in train a vigorous revolutionary movement in Bohemia which eventually led to the Hussite Wars. Notable among the many memorials to the Reformer are the statues in Old Town Square and in the grand courtyard of the Carolinum. Adjoining the Bethlehem Chapel is a reconstruction of the house in which he lived.

John of Nepomuk took orders in 1370, and in 1380 was ordained as a priest. After studying law in Prague and Padua he was appointed Vicar-General of the archdiocese of Prague.
In 1393, on the orders of King Wenceslas IV, he was arrested, tortured and thrown in chains from the Charles Bridge into the Vltava: according to legend because he had refused to reveal to the King the secret of the Queen's confession, but according to the historians because he had appointed an abbot of Kladruby Abbey against the King's wishes. He was canonised in 1729 and became Patron Saint of Bohemia.
There are several statues of St John of Nepomuk in Prague. Perhaps the best known is the one on the Charles Bridge, erected in 1683 and soon followed by 29 other statues of saints.
John of Nepomuk is the best-known bridge-saint in Europe. He is invoked against danger from water and unjust suspicion. His normal attributes are a crown of five stars (representing the five lights which were said to have appeared over the spot where he was drowned), a crucifix, biretta and rochet.

St John of Nepomuk
(c. 1350–1393)

The writings of Franz Kafka, an insurance clerk by profession, attracted little attention in his lifetime. His novels ("America", "The Trial", "The Castle") and many of his short stories were published after his death by Max Brod, against his express wishes.
After the Second World War Kafka's work became the subject of international interest, and theologians and Communists, psychologists, philosophers and existentialists all sought their own interpretations of his very personal world. Two of his novels, "The Castle" and "The Trial", were made into films.
There is a bust of Kafka in Old Town Square. He is buried in the New Jewish Cemetery.

Franz Kafka
Prague writer
(1883–1924)

Notable Personalities

Charles IV
King of Bohemia and
Holy Roman Emperor
(1316–78)

Charles became King of Bohemia in 1346 and Emperor in 1355. He founded Prague's University (the Carolinum) and built the Charles Bridge, St Vitus's Cathedral, the New Town of Prague and Karlštejn Castle, the last named as a place of safety in which to keep the Imperial insignia and Crown Jewels.

Charles made Prague the capital of the Empire, the "Rome of the North". During his reign poets such as Petrarch and Rienzo came to Prague and there was a great flowering of architecture. Charles himself was a writer, the author of the "Legend of St Wenceslas", the "Fürstenspiegel" ("Mirror of Princes") and the "Vita Caroli" (see Quotations).

Johannes Kepler
German astronomer
(1571–1630)

When Johannes Kepler was compelled to leave Graz during the Counter-Reformation he moved to Prague, where he succeeded Tycho Brahe as Court Astronomer to the Emperor Rudolf II in 1601. On the basis of Brahe's observations he formulated the laws governing the motion of the planets.

Kepler also did pioneering work in the field of optics and invented the astronomical telescope. After the death of Rudolf II he left Prague and moved to Linz.

Egon Erwin Kisch
Czech journalist and writer
(1885–1948)

Egon Erwin Kisch achieved a considerable reputation as an active and vigorous reporter. His early years in Prague provided the material for works such as "Prague Adventures" and "Tales from Prague's Streets and Nights".

There is a commemorative plaque on the house in which he was born, U dvou zlatých medvědů ("At the Sign of the Two Golden Bears") in the Old Town (Kožná 475/1).

Josef Mánes
Czech painter
(1820–71)

Josef Mánes, originally influenced by the ideas of the Romantic school, is regarded as the founder of Czech landscape-painting and of a school of national folk-painting, to which he gave monumental scale. In 1848 he took an active part in the Czech Rising. His realistic paintings and illustrations (to folk-songs) depict country folk as ideal representatives of the people, and his cycle of the months on the astronomical clock in Old Town Square shows scenes of peasant life (originals in the staircase hall of the Municipal Museum).

There are pictures by Mánes in the Mánes Exhibition Hall and St Agnes's Convent. He is commemorated by a monument at the end of Mánes Bridge.

Wolfgang Amadeus Mozart
Austrian composer
(1756–91)

While the first performance of Mozart's "Figaro" in Vienna (1786) was a failure, its first performance in Prague was greeted with enthusiasm. "The good people of Prague understand me," declared the composer.

In October 1787 "Don Giovanni" was given its first performance in the Old Town Theatre (now the Tyl Theatre), and in 1791 Mozart wrote "La Clemenza di Tito" for the Emperor Leopold's coronation as King of Bohemia.

Mozart had many friends in Prague, and was on intimate terms with the music teacher F. X. Dušek and his wife Josephine. There is a Mozart Museum in their villa, the Bertramka, in Prague-Smíchov.

Alfons Mucha
Czech artist
(1860–1939)

The graphic artist and designer Alfons Mucha worked for a time as a scene-painter in Vienna, and then studied art in Munich and from 1888 in Paris, where he made a name for himself particularly with his posters for the actress Sarah Bernhardt. He also worked on interior decoration, applied art and book

W. A. Mozart

Bedřich Smetana

Wallenstein

illustration. He was a major influence on the Jugendstil (Art Nouveau) movement. After spending some years in America (1904–10) he returned to Czechoslovakia. He is buried in Vyšehrad Castle.

As a historian František Palacký saw the Hussite period as a central phase in Czech history. In 1848 he refused to take part in the German National Assembly in Frankfurt and presided over the Pan-Slav Congress in Prague, becoming a leading figure in the movement for the revival of Czech national feeling. There is a monument to him at the Palacký Bridge in the New Town.

František Palacký
Czech historian and politician
(1798–1876)

The German architect and sculptor Peter Parler played a major part in the development of Gothic art in Central Europe.
In 1353 he was summoned to Prague by Charles IV to continue work on St Vitus's Cathedral. He built All Saints Chapel in the Castle and designed the Charles Bridge, with the Old Town Bridge Tower, the sculpture on which also came from his workshop. His sons Wenzel and Johann carried on the construction of the Cathedral. His nephew Heinrich worked in Prague as a sculptor.

Peter Parler
German architect and sculptor
(1330–99)

Benedikt Ried von Piesting was one of the principal representatives of Late Gothic architecture in Bohemia, the supreme exponent of the vaulted architecture of the Pre-Renaissance. He designed the Vladislav Hall in the Royal Palace in Hradčany Castle, one of the most magnificent secular buildings of its day.

Benedikt Ried von Piesting
Bohemian architect
(c. 1454–1534)

Rilke was born in the Herrengasse in Prague. After a brief career as an officer, ended on health grounds, he studied art, philosophy and literature in Prague, Munich and Berlin. Many of his works were written under the influence of the Prague milieu of his day, a declining world of aristocratic and middle-class culture.

Rainer Maria Rilke
Prague poet
(1875–1926)

Smetana studied piano and musical theory in Prague and established his own music school there in 1848. After five years in Sweden he returned to his native city in 1861, and in 1866 became Conductor of the National Theatre Orchestra. He

Bedřich Smetana
Czech composer
(1824–84)

Notable Personalities

founded a Czech national style in both opera ("The Bartered Bride") and symphonic music ("Vltava"). Although he became deaf at the age of 50 he did not give up composition. He died in an asylum.

Smetana is buried in the cemetery in Vyšehrad Castle. There is a Smetana Museum at Novotného lávka 1 in the Old Town.

Wallenstein
Imperial General in
Thirty Years War
(1583–1634)

Albrecht Wenzel Eusebius von Waldstein (Valdštejn), better known as Wallenstein, was one of the great generals of the Thirty Years War. Accused of plotting high treason, he was dismissed and outlawed by the Emperor, and in 1634 was murdered together with his closest associates.

The Waldstein (Valdštejn) Palace in the Lesser Quarter was Prague's first Baroque palace.

St Wenceslas (Václav)
Duke of Bohemia
(c. 903–929 or 935)

Wenceslas became Duke of Bohemia in 921. His grandmother and teacher, St Ludmilla, was killed by his mother Drahomira on religious grounds, and Wenceslas himself was murdered by his brother, Boleslav the Cruel, in 929 or 935.

Legend and reports of miracles made Wenceslas the country's national saint.

In Wenceslas Square, in front of the National Museum, is an equestrian statue of the saint with other national saints – Procopius, Ludmilla, Adalbert and Agnes. In the beautiful Wenceslas Chapel in Hradčany Castle can be seen a door-ring in the form of a lion's head to which Wenceslas is said to have clung when attacked by his brother.

Franz Werfel
Prague writer
(1890–1945)

Franz Werfel ranked with Brod, Kafka and Kisch as one of the great Prague writers of his day. He began by writing lyric poetry in the Expressionist manner and Symbolist dramas of ideas, but later turned to historical and political realism. His best-known works are the drama "Der Spiegelmensch" ("The Mirror Man"), "Der jüngste Tag" ("The Last Judgment"), a collection of poems, and the novels "Die vierzig Tage des Musa Dagh" ("The Forty Days of Musa Dagh"), "Die veruntreute Himmel" ("The Embezzled Heaven") and "Stern der Ungeborenen" ("Star of the Unborn").

History of Prague

Various tribes move from their heartland in Bohemia through the Vltava hills into the area now occupied by Prague.	4000 B.C.
A trading settlement is established at the ford on the Vltava below the Hradčany, where the Amber road and the Salt road intersect.	3000–1000 B.C.
The Boii, a Celtic people, move into Bohemia.	From 400 B.C.
The Boii are subjugated by the Marcomanni, a Germanic tribe.	10 B.C.
During the Great Migrations Western Slavs occupy the Prague area, with settlements on the castle hill and in what is now the Lesser Quarter.	6th c. A.D.
Prague now consists of a number of fortified settlements. Legend has it that Prague was founded by Libuše, a princess with the gift of divination. When the people tired of this feminine rule she sent her henchmen into the forest, telling them to establish a town at the spot where they saw a ploughman (*přemysl*) constructing the threshold (*práh*) of a house. This is the traditional explanation of the names of the Přemyslid dynasty and of Prague.	800
Duke Bořivoj, the first historically attested member of the Přemyslid dynasty, conquers the Czech tribes. The castle of Prague, the Hradčany, is built.	c. 850–95
Bořivoj is baptised by Methodius, the Apostle of the Slaves. After his death his wife Ludmilla, also a Christian, is murdered. She becomes Bohemia's first martyr and patron saint.	874
Wenceslas, Ludmilla's grandson, becomes Duke of Bohemia.	921
Wenceslas is murdered by his brother Boleslav the Cruel (Boleslav I).	929 (or 935)
During the reign of Boleslav II, the Pious, the episcopal see of Prague is established. The territory of Bohemia now extends to the boundaries of Kievan Russia.	973
Jewish, German, Italian and French merchants settle in Prague.	900–1000
St Adalbert, Bishop of Prague, founds the Benedictine Abbey of Břevnov.	993
Duke Vradislav II (from 1085 King Vradislav I) transfers his residence from the Hradčany to the Vyšehrad.	1061–92
Duke Vladislav II is proclaimed King of Bohemia. With the construction of the first stone bridge over the Vltava (later replaced by the Charles Bridge) Prague establishes its lasting dominance as a centre of trade.	1158

1178	Duke Soběslav II grants German merchants the right to be dealt with by German law, exemption from military service and fiscal privileges in order to encourage them to stay in Prague.
1198	The Emperor raises the Duke of Bohemia (Přemysl Ottokar I) to the status of King.
c. 1230	Prague is fortified and receives its municipal charter.
1257	King Přemysl Ottokar II establishes the Lesser Quarter (Malá Strana) as a German settlement governed by the Magdeburg legal code. Ottokar extends his kingdom to include Austria and large territories in northern Italy, but is unsuccessful in his attempt to become Emperor.
c. 1300	The Prague groschen begins to be minted (63 groschen= 1 mark). It circulates widely in Germany and becomes the model for the German groschen.
1306	With the murder of King Wenceslas III the Přemyslid dynasty dies out.
1310	The German King Henry VII, of the House of Luxemburg, marries his son Johann to Elisabeth, heiress of the Přemyslid dynasty, and thus secures the throne of Bohemia for his family.
1344	Charles IV rules Bohemia. Work begins on the construction of St Vitus's Cathedral, the archiepiscopal church of the newly created archdiocese of Prague.
1346	Charles IV becomes King of Bohemia.
1347	Charles becomes German King. He makes Bohemia the heartland of the Empire and unites Bohemia, Moravia and Silesia under the Bohemian Crown. As capital of the Holy Roman Empire Prague becomes the "Rome of the North". Scholars and artists flock to the city from all over Europe.
1348	Foundation of the Charles University, the first university in Central Europe. The development of the New Town, mainly to house tradesmen and craftsmen, makes Prague the largest city in Central Europe, in both area and population. Charles builds the Church of St Mary of the Snows and Karlštejn Castle.
1355	Charles IV becomes Holy Roman Emperor.
1356	Charles establishes the precedence of the kings of Bohemia over other lay Electors in the Golden Bull.
1357	Construction of the Charles Bridge and the Old Town Bridge Tower.
1378–1419	During the reign of Wenceslas IV there are severe social and religious tensions and conflicts over the throne. In 1400 Wenceslas is deposed as German King but remains King of Bohemia.

On the urging of Jan Hus, Wenceslas curtails the rights of Germans in the universities, and 2000 German students and many professors leave the country. 1409

Jan Hus, appearing before the Council of Constance, refuses to retract his beliefs and is burned at the stake. His death triggers off a national anti-Church movement in Bohemia. 1415

First Defenestration of Prague: a mob storms the New Town Hall, frees Hussites imprisoned there and two Catholic councillors are thrown out of the window.
Beginning of the Hussite Wars. Death of Wenceslas IV. 1419

Pope Martin V issues a Bull proclaiming a crusade against heretics in Bohemia. The Hussite army, led by Jan Žižka, defeats King Sigismund's crusading army in the Battle of Veitsburg.
Thereafter the Hussites, led by Prokop the Elder, take the offensive and mount retaliatory campaigns in Bavaria, Brandenburg, Saxony and Austria. Although they lose the war they gain some of their demands (expropriation of the Church's secular property, use of the chalice in Communion). 1420

Under the rule of George of Poděbrad (who becomes King of Bohemia in 1458) building activity continues in Prague. The princes, enriched by the expropriation of Church property, win increased influence. Prague's importance as a trading centre declines. 1436–71

The domains of the Bohemian Crown are united with Poland and Hungary. King Vladislav Jagiello transfers the capital from Prague to Buda. 1490

The Bohemian Crown falls to Ferdinand I, a Habsburg. 1526

German Lutherans settle in Prague, reinforcing the opposition to the Counter-Reformation now introduced to Bohemia by the Roman Catholic Habsburgs. From 1549

Ferdinand I becomes Emperor. He summons the Jesuits to Prague. 1556

Rudolf II is attacked by his nephew Leopold and is compelled to appeal to his brother Matthias and the Bohemian Estates for help. In return he concedes freedom of religion to the nobility. 1609

Rudolf II abdicates and his brother Matthias becomes King. 1612

The Second Defenestration of Prague is the signal for a rising by the radical Protestant nobility against the Habsburgs. Beginning of the Thirty Years War. 1618

The Bohemian Estates depose the Habsburg Ferdinand II and choose Elector Frederick V of the Palatinate as King. 1619

Frederick II defeats Frederick V, the "Winter King", in the Battle of the White Mountain and establishes his hereditary right to the throne. 1620

1621	Twenty-seven leaders of the rising of the nobility are executed in the Old Town. The Protestant aristocracy is deprived of all power.
1624	Ferdinand II moves the Bohemian Court Chancellery to Vienna, and Bohemia is ruled by officials responsible to Vienna. German and Czech remain the official languages, with equal status, but Czech gives place to German as a literary language.
1627	An Imperial Ordinance establishes the hereditary right of the House of Austria to the throne of Bohemia. Catholicism is the only permitted religion. The monarch has the pre-eminent right to legislate, appoint high dignitaries and annul resolutions of the Landtag (Diet). The power of the Estates is finally destroyed by this new constitutional law for Bohemia and Moravia, which remains in force until the 19th c.
1631	Wallenstein drives back the Swedes, who in the course of the Thirty Years War have advanced to the gates of Prague.
1648	The news of the end of the war comes just as the Swedes are occupying the Lesser Quarter. The Thirty Years War has catastrophic effects on Bohemia. Prague loses all cultural and economic importance.
1741–42	During the War of the Austrian Succession Prague is occupied by Bavarian and Austrian forces.
1757	During the Seven Years War Frederick the Great defeats the Austrians at Prague, but raises the siege of the city after his defeat at Kolín.
1781	Joseph II, continuing a process of reform begun in 1680, abolishes serfdom. The use of the German language is further promoted.
1784	The Hradčany, Lesser Quarter, Old Town and New Town are combined to form a single unit.
1845	Opening of the railway between Prague and Vienna.
1848	A Czech national rising centred on Prague is crushed. František Palacký refuses to take part in the German National Assembly in Frankfurt. The Pan-Slav Congress meets in Prague. Increased tensions between Germans and Czechs.
1861	The Germans lose their majority in the Prague municipal parliament for the first time.
1882	Prague University is divided up according to nationality.
1886	The German members of the Landtag withdraw. The movement of Czechs into towns of predominantely German population produces a change in ethnic structure, but the Germans still maintain their economic predominance.
1891	Industrial Exhibition in Prague. Industrialisation, particularly in areas of German settlement, has made Bohemia an industrial heartland of the Danube Monarchy.

Tensions between Germans and Czechs reduce the Landtag to impotence. During the First World War a state of emergency is declared in Bohemia. 1913

Establishment of the Czechoslovak Republic, one of the Slav successor States to the Austro-Hungarian Monarchy. The first President is Tomáš G. Masaryk. 1918
The new multi-racial State is threatened by constant tensions between the various national groups (Czechs, Slovaks, Germans, Hungarians, Poles).

Munich agreement: the German-settled territories of the Czechoslovak Republic are incorporated in Hitler's Germany. 1938

The rest of Czechoslovakia becomes the Protectorate of Bohemia and Moravia, under Nazi rule. 1939

After the end of the Second World War Zdeněk Fierlinger, a Social Democrat, proclaims the Košice Programme for a state on Socialist principles. 1945

The Communist Party (KPČ) assumes power. Czechoslovakia becomes a People's Republic. 1948

Establishment of the Czechoslovak Socialist Republic (ČSSR). 1960

The "Prague Spring", under President Svoboda and First Secretary Dubček, is brought to an end by the intervention of Warsaw Pact troops. The Soviet Union gains the right to maintain troops in Czechoslovakia for an indefinite period. 1968

The city is considerably enlarged by the incorporation of rural areas on the outskirts. The first Underground (Metro) line comes into operation. 1974

The modern Palace of Culture is opened. 1981

Quotations

Charles IV
King of Bohemia
Holy Roman Emperor
(1316–78)
"Vita Caroli"

"Finally we came back to Bohemia after eleven years of absence. Our mother Elisabeth we found no longer alive: she had died some years before. And so we found, on our arrival in Bohemia, neither father nor mother, nor brother nor sisters, nor any other acquaintance.

"We had, too, quite forgotten the Bohemian language. Later, however, we recovered our command of it.

"This kingdom had fallen on evil days. No single castle was free; they had all been put in pawn, along with all the possesssions of the crown, so that we had no place to stay, save in a house in the town like any other burgher. The castle of Prague had been so devastated, dilapidated and destroyed since the time of Ottokar that it had been wholly levelled to the ground. There we ordered the building, at heavy cost, of the spacious and stately palace.

"All honest Bohemians loved us, for they knew that we were a scion of the old royal house of Bohemia, and lent us their help in the recovery of the castles and the royal domains."

Wilhelm von Humboldt
German traveller and
scientist
(1769–1859)

". . . the most beautiful inland town in Europe."

Patrick Leigh Fermor
English writer
(b. 1915)
"A Time of Gifts"
(referring to a journey in
1933)

"A first glance, then, reveals a Baroque city loaded with the spoils of the Austrian Caesars. It celebrates the Habsburg marriage-claims to the crown of Bohemia and reaffirms the questionable supersession of the old elective rights of the Bohemians; and alongside the Emperor's temporal ascendancy, this architecture symbolises the triumph of the Pope's Imperial champion over the Hussites and the Protestants. Some of the churches bear witness to the energy of the Jesuits. They are stone emblems of their fierce zeal in the religious conflict. . . .

"But in spite of this scene, a renewed scrutiny of the warren below reveals an earlier and a medieval city where squat towers jut. A russet-scaled labyrinth of late medieval roofs embeds the Baroque splendours. Barn-like slants of tiles open their rows of flat dormers like gills – a medieval ventilation device for the breeze to dry laundry after those rare washing-days. Robust buildings join each other over arcades that are stayed by the slant of heavy buttresses. Coloured houses erupt at street corners in the cupola-topped cylinders and octagons that I had first admired in Swabia, and the façades and the gables are decorated with pediments and scrolls and steps; teams of pargetted men and animals process solemnly round the walls; and giants in high relief look as though they are half immured and trying to elbow their way out. Hardly a street is untouched by religious bloodshed; every important square has been a ceremonious stage for beheadings.

"The symbolic carved chalices, erased from strongholds of the Utraquist sect of the Hussites – who claimed communion in both kinds for the laity – were replaced by the Virgin's statue after the re-establishment of Catholicism. Steel spikes, clustered about with minor spires, rise by the score from the belfries of the older churches and the steeples of the river

Franz Grillparzer

Detlev von Liliencron

Thomas Mann

barbicans, flattened into sharp wedges, are encased in metal scales and set about with spikes and balls and iron pennants. These are armourers' rather than masons' work. They look like engines meant to lame or hamstring infernal cavalry after dark. Streets rise abruptly; lanes turn the corners in fans of steps; and the cobbles are steep enough to bring down dray-horses and send toboggans out of control. . . .

"These spires and towers recalled the earlier Prague of the Wenceslases and the Ottokars and the race of the Přemysl kings, sprung from the fairy-tale marriage of a Czech princess with a plough-boy encountered on the banks of the river. . . ."

"On the West side of the Molda is the Emperours Castle, seated on a most high Mountaine, in the fall whereof is the Suburbe called Kleinseit, or little side. From this Suburbe to goe into the City, a long stone bridge is to be passed over Molda, which runnes from the South to the North, and divides the suburbe from the City, to which as you goe, on the left side is the little City of the Jewes, compassed with wals, and before your eies towards the East, is the City called new Prage, both which Cities are compassed about with a third, called old Prage. So as Prage consists of three Cities, all compassed with wals, yet is nothing lesse then strong, and except the stinch of the streets drive back the Turkes, or they meet them in open field, there is small hope in the fortifications thereof."

Fynes Moryson
English traveller
(1566–1630)
"An Itinerary", 1617

"All in all, Prague is one of the finest and most picturesque cities on the continent, much more interesting than Berlin or any other German capital. The extraordinary historical treasures of Prague make the city worth the closest observation. It would be a foolish enterprise to write a history of the world without previously visiting this ancient capital."

Charles Sealsfield
(real name Karl Anton Postl)
Moravian writer
(1793–1864)

"There stood on a crag on the banks of the Moldau, before its waters reached Prague, the Castle of Vyšehrad. It was built when primeval forest still covered all these hills on the Moldau, long before the hero Zaboy lived and the singer Lumir. And then came Krok and had his golden residence in the sacred castle. Then there was Libuša, who among all her sisters was his favourite child, and she married the ploughman Přemysl and caused the first wooden stake for the Castle of Prague to be

Adalbert Stifter
Austrian writer
(1805–68)
"Witiko" (a historical novel)

25

hewn. And from her there came numerous descendants, and they ruled over the peoples. One of them had himself baptised after Christ was born and brought the holy faith into the world. He was called Duke Bořivoj. His grandson was St Wenceslas and his wife St Ludmilla. He built the first church in Bohemia in his Castle of Hradec. Then at once he built the Church of the Blessed Virgin Mary in the Castle of Prague. In this church Duke Vladislav celebrated the cutting off of the hair of his son, St Wenceslas, and to this day it brings salvation to all believers. There, too, is the high Church of St Vitus. It was built with great labour and pains. St Wenceslas built it, and the Bishop of Regensburg, Tuto, granted him permission. Then Bishop Tuto died, and he who came after him, Bishop Michael, consecrated the church. It glowed with gold and silver and was full of splendour. And since it was too small Duke Spytihněv pulled it down and rebuilt it much larger, and then it was burned down and rebuilt again, and then lightning destroyed the tower and the tower was built anew. The most sacred treasures are in it. The German King gave St Wenceslas an arm of St Vitus for the church. Then the body of St Wenceslas himself was buried in it, and since that time many wonders have come about. And the body of the holy martyr Adalbert rests in it, and his vestments are preserved in its treasury, and the body of martyr Podiven, the faithful servant of St Wenceslas, is buried in it, and the body of Radim, the brother of St Adalbert. The church cannot accommodate the host of worshippers when it is the Feast of St Wenceslas and the sick come from foreign lands to be cured and when the Feast of St Adalbert is celebrated. This church is the most sacred church in the whole land of Bohemia. Then there is also the Church of St George. It was built still earlier than the Church of St Vitus. It was built by Duke Vladislav, son of the Duke Bořivoj who was baptised and father of St Wenceslas. Then he was buried in it, and the body of his mother, the holy martyr Ludmilla, also rests there. Beside it is the convent of the pious women of St George, where now the wounded are cared for.''

Sights from A to Z

Adria Building

See Cloth Hall

Archbishop's Palace

See Hradčany Square

Artists' House (Dům umělců)   C4(F/G9)

Location
Náměští Krásnoarmějců
(Red Army Square), Staré
Mešto, Praha 1

Metro
Staroměstská

Buses
133, 144, 156

Tram
17

Artists' House is now the home of the Czech Philharmonic Orchestra (Česká Filharmonie). Concerts are given here, particularly during the internationally known Prague Spring Festival (May–June).

The Building, erected in 1876–84, was designed by Josef Zítek and Josef Schulz, the architects responsible for the National Theatre (see entry). It was originally called the Rudolfinum, after Crown Prince Rudolf of Austria, and is still familiarly referred to by that name.

Artists' House ranks with the National Theatre and the National Museum (see entry) as one of Prague's finest neo-Renaissance buildings. It was occupied from 1919 to 1939 by the Parliament of the Czechoslovaks and by a picture gallery which was later moved to the gallery in Hradčany Castle (see entry).

Belvedere Palace (Královský letohrádek)   C4

Location
Hradčany, Praha 1

Metro
Malostranská

Tram
22

Opening times
Tues.–Sun. 10 a.m.–6 p.m.

This splendid pleasure palace was built by Ferdinand I for his wife Anna at the same time as he laid out the Royal Gardens (1538–63).

The arcaded building in the style of the Italian Renaissance with its gracefully curving roof was designed by Paolo della Stella. The upper floor was not completed until 1564.

The external colonnade is decorated with a frieze of foliage ornament and reliefs depicting scenes from Greek mythology and a likeness of Ferdinand I presenting a flower to his wife. The figures of divinities at the entrance are by Matthias Braun (c. 1730).

The Great Hall has frescoes by the Historical painter Christian Ruben (d. 1875). This room is frequently used for exhibitions. From the balcony there is a magnificent view of the Hradčany (see entry) and the city.

To the west of the Belvedere is the Singing Fountain (bronze, cast by Tomáš Jaroš in 1564).

To the south of the palace are the Chotek Gardens.

The Renaissance-style Belvedere Palace

Bertramka (Mozart Museum)

Location
Mozartova 2/169, Smíchov,
Praha 5

Trams
4, 9, 15

In this suburban villa (originally 17th c., rebuilt in the 18th) Mozart stayed with his friends the Dušeks during his frequent visits to Prague. Here he completed "Don Giovanni", which was given its first performance in 1787 in what was then the Theatre of the Estates and is now the Tyl Theatre.

The Bertramka now houses the Mozart Museum. Concerts are frequently given here.

Opening times are Tues.–Fri. 2–5 p.m. and Sat. and Sun. 9 a.m.–5 p.m.

Bethlehem Chapel (Betlémska kaple)　　　C5(G10)

Location
Betlémské náměstí
(Bethlehem Square), Staré
Město, Praha 1

Metro
Staroměstská, Můstek

Trams
5, 9, 19, 22

Opening times
Apr.–Sep. 9 a.m.–6 p.m.
Oct.–Mar. 9 a.m.–5 p.m.

The Bethlehem Chapel was rebuilt in its original form in 1950–54, with the help of old descriptions and views.

In 1391 the burghers of Prague wanted to build a church in which the Mass would be said in Czech, but the Roman Catholic authorities agreed only to the construction of a chapel – though in the event it was a chapel which could accommodate a congregation of 3000 and was centred on the pulpit rather than the altar.

The Czech Reformer Jan Hus preached here between 1402 and 1413; he is commemorated by a memorial house adjoining the chapel. After his death the chapel remained the spiritual centre of the Hussite movement. In 1521 the German peasant leader

Thomas Münzer proclaimed from the pulpit his vision of a communistic state and issued his Prague Manifesto.
After the Battle of the White Mountain (1621) in which Ferdinand II defeated the "Winter King", Frederick V of the Palatinate, and the Ordinance of 1627 declaring Catholicism the only permitted faith the chapel was acquired by the Jesuits. In 1781 it was pulled down, leaving only the foundations.
The rebuilding of the chapel was justified by Prime Minister Klement Gottwald on the ground that "five hundred years ago the people of Prague were already fighting for Communism".

Bilá Hora

See White Mountain

Botanic Garden (Botanická zahrada)   C/D7

The Botanic Garden has a tradition going back 600 years, and displays a corresponding variety of both native and exotic plants.
The garden was laid out during the reign of Charles IV by a Florentine apothecary named Angelo. The University Garden, established in Smíchov in 1775, was transferred to this site in 1897.

Location
Ulice Na slupi,
Nové Město, Praha 1

Trams
18, 24

Břevnov Abbey (Bývalý benediktinský klášter)

5 km (3 miles) from the city centre on the Karlovy Vary road (No. 6) is the district of Břevnov, with a former Benedictine abbey founded by St Adalbert in 993 – the oldest monastery in Bohemia.

Courtyard
The courtyard is entered through a handsome gateway designed by Kilian Ignaz Dientzenhofer (1740).
In the courtyard can be seen a statue of St Benedict by Karl Josef Hiernle.

Conventual buildings
The Baroque conventual buildings were begun by Paul Ignaz Bayer in 1708 and completed about 1715 by Christoph Dientzenhofer. They now house the Central Archives of Prague. The fine Prelates' Hall has a ceiling-fresco by Cosmas Damian Asam (St Günther's miracle of the peacock, 1727).

St Margaret's Church
The central element in the abbey is St Margaret's Church (Kostel svaté Markéty), which was also built by Christoph Dientzenhofer (completed c. 1720). The ceiling-frescoes are by Johann Jakob Steinfels, the altar-pieces by Peter Brandl. The statue of St Margaret on the high alter is by Matthäus Wenzel Jäckel. In front of the church stands a statue of St John of Nepomuk by K. J. Hiernle.

Location
Merkétská ulice,
Břevnov, Praha 6

Buses
108, 174, 180, 237

Trams
8, 22, 23

Buquoy Palace (Buquoyský palác) C5

Location
Velkopřevorské náměstí,
Malá Strana, Praha 1

Trams
12, 22

The Buquoy Palace, now the French Embassy, was built in 1628, probably to the design of Jean-Baptiste Mathey, and rebuilt in 1738. The staircase, in neo-Renaissance style, dates from 1889–96, and further alterations were made in 1904. The neo-Baroque interior decoration dates from 1860. The old palace gardens, left in their natural state, extend down to Kampa Island (see entry).

Carolinum (Karolinum) D5(G10)

Location
Železná 9,
Staré Město, Praha 1

Metro
Můstek

Trams
5, 9, 19, 29

The Carolinum was founded by Charles IV in 1348 – the first university in Central Europe. The original nucleus of the building was the Röthlow House, donated for the purpose by Wenceslas IV in 1383, the superb Gothic oriel of which is still preserved. Soon, however, the history of the Carolinum as a university in the true sense, open to teachers and students from all over Europe, seemed to come to an end when, in 1409, Wenceslas gave way to the urging of the Reformer Jan Hus and curtailed the rights of Germans in the university, whereupon 2000 students and many professors left. Thereafter Hus (statue by J. Lidičky in the Grand Courtyard) ruled the university as Rector, until in 1412 the Catholic faculty denounced him and he was compelled to flee to southern Bohemia. After the suppression of the rising by the Bohemian nobility the university was taken over the by the Jesuits.

Gothic oriel of the Carolinum

Of the original building there survive, in addition to the oriel, only the foundations and a few recently exposed Gothic features. The rest was remodelled in Baroque style by F. M. Kaňka in 1718.
The heart of the Carolinum is the large Assembly Hall (17th c.), two storeys high, which was extended in 1946–50.

Celetná ulice (Bakers' Street)   D5(G/H10)

This street, named after the bakers who baked rolls (*calty*) here in the Middle Ages, was from time immemorial a route from the Vltava ford and the market-place of the Old Town to the east. This, too, was the route followed by the royal coronation procession from the Powder Tower (see entry) by way of Old Town Square and the Charles Bridge (see entries) to the Castle (see Hradčany).
The Street is lined for most of its length by handsome old palaces of Romanesque or Gothic origin, rebuilt in the Baroque period. One of the finest is the former Hrzán Palace (No. 12), which is believed to have been remodelled in High Baroque style by G. B. Alliprandi in 1702.

Location
Staré Město, Praha 1

Metro
Staroměstská, Můstek

Trams
3, 5, 9, 10, 26, 29

Charles Bridge (Karlův most)   C5(F10)

The Charles Bridge (closed to motor vehicles) spans the Vltava, linking the Old Town (Staré Město) and the Lesser Quarter (Malá Strana). From the bridge there are marvellous views of the Vltava Valley with its numerous bridges, the Žofín and Střelecký islands, the Old Town and the Lesser Quarter, dominated by Hradčany Castle (see entry). Under the western piers lies Kampa Island (see entry), separated from the Lesser Quarter by the Čertovka ("Little Venice"), a narrow arm of the river.
The bridge, supported on 16 piers, is 520 m (570 yd) long and 10 m (33 ft) wide. It was begun by Peter Parler and J. Ottl in 1357, during the reign of Charles IV, but not completed until the reign of Wenceslas IV, in the early 15th c. The massive towers at each end, like the bridge itself, were designed for defence.
Devastating floods have frequently damaged the bridge – in 1890, for example, two arches had to be rebuilt – but it has never collapsed.

Location
Staré Město, Praha 1

Metro
Staroměstská, Malostranská

Buses
133, 144, 156

Trams
12, 17, 22

"An avenue of statues"
The Charles Bridge achieves its powerful effect mainly through its rich sculptural decoration. This "avenue of statues", as it has been called, is mainly a product of the Baroque period; it is one of Prague's finest Baroque architectural compositions, and forms a remarkably effective combination with the severely Gothic structure of the bridge itself.
A bronze Crucifix which had stood here since the 14th c. was renewed in 1657, and between 1706 and 1714 26 pieces of sculpture by leading artists of the day (Matthias Bernhard Braun, Johann Brokoff and his sons Michael Josef and Ferdinand Maximilian) and other sculptors were set up on the bridge; these were followed in the mid 19th c. by five other pieces of sculpture (Josef Max and Emanuel Max); and in 1938 the group by Karel Dvořák representing St Cyril and St

31

Charles Bridge

Lesser Quarter
Bridge Towers

Statues

→ N

St Wenceslas
by J. K. Böhm, 1858

SS. Cosmas and Damian
by J. O. Mayer, 1709

SS. John of Matha, Felix of Valois
and Ivan and figure of a Turk
by F. M. Brokoff, 1714

St Vitus
by F. M. Brokoff, 1714 (marble)

St Adalbert
by F. M. Brokoff, 1709 (copy, 1973)

St Philip Benizi
by M. B. Mandl, 1714

St Luitgard
by M. B. Braun, 1710

St Cajetan
by F. M. Brokoff, 1709

St Nicholas of Tolentino
by J. F. Kohl, 1706 (copy, 1969)

St Augustine
by J. F. Kohl, 1708
(copy, 1974)

SS. Vincent Ferrer and Procopius
by F. M. Brokoff, 1712

St Jude Thaddaeus
by J. O. Mayer, 1708

Roland Column
(originally 16th c.;
copy of 1884)

St Francis Seraphicus
by E. Max, 1855

St Anthony of Padua
by J. O. Mayer, 1707

SS. Ludmilla and Wenceslas
workshop of M. B. Braun, c. 1730

St John of Nepomuk
by M. Rauchmüller and J. Brokoff,
1683; cast in bronze by W. H. Heroldt,
Nuremberg, 1683

St Francis Borgia
by J. amd F. M. Brokoff, 1710
(restored by R. Vlach, 1937)

SS. Wenceslas, Norbert and
Sigismund
by J. Max, 1853

St Christopher
by E. Max, 1857

St John the Baptist
by J. Max, 1857

St Francis Xavier
by F. M. Brokoff, 1711 (copy, 1913)

SS. Cyril and Methodius and three
allegorical figures (Bohemia,
Moravia and Slovakia),
by K. Dvořák, 1938

St Joseph
by J. Max, 1854

St Anne with the Virgin and Child
by M. W. Jäckel, 1707

Pietà
by E. Max, 1859 (originally 1695)

Bronze Crucifix
cast by J. Hilger, 1629; the first piece
of sculpture on the bridge, set up
1657; Hebrew inscription of 1696;
figures by E. Max, 1861

SS. Barbara, Margaret and
Elizabeth
by F. M. Brokoff, 1707

Virgin with SS. Dominic and
Thomas Aquinas
by M. W. Jäckel, 1709 (copy, 1961)

St Ivo
by M. B. Braun, 1711 (copy, 1908)

Virgin with St Bernard
by M. W. Jäckel, 1709 (copy)

Old Town Bridge
Tower

The **Charles Bridge** was begun
in 1357 by Peter Parler, but
completed only at the beginning
of the 15th c. Its irregular course
is probably due to the fact that
after the collapse in 1342 of the
first stone bridge over the Vltava
(the Judith Bridge, built between
1158 and 1172), new piers were
set beside the old ones but the
original bridgeheads were re-
used.

Sculpture on the Charles Bridge: The Virgin with St Bernard (left) and St John of Nepomuk (right)

Methodius was added. The sandstone of the statues has suffered badly from the weather, and they are gradually being replaced by copies. The only marble figure is that of St Philip Benizi.

The finest figure is that of St Luitgard, the very image of mercy and compassion. Christ is shown bending down from the cross towards the Saint and permitting her to kiss his wounds.

The only bronze statue is that of St John of Nepomuk, in the middle of the bridge, which was cast in Nuremberg in 1683 after models by Matthias and Rauchmüller and Johann Brokoff. Between the sixth and seventh piers of the bridge is a relief carving, marking the spot where St John of Nepomuk was thrown into the Vltava in 1393 on the order of Wenceslas IV because he had taken sides against the King in an ecclesiastical conflict. John of Nepomuk was canonised in 1729, and has been regarded since then as the "bridge-saint" of Catholic Europe.

On the Crucifixion group is a tablet with a Hebrew inscription, set up here by a Jew who was ordered by the court in 1695 to make this reparation for abusing Christ.

The Old Town Bridge Tower, built on the first of the piers, forms the eastern access to the bridge. It was begun in 1391 and completed in the early 15th c. (to the design of Peter Parler) by the Cathedral workshop. It is rated the finest Gothic tower in Central Europe, with figural decoration which ranks among the master works of Gothic sculpture in Bohemia (14th c.). On the east side, at the top, are statues of the patron saints of Bohemia, St Adalbert and St Sigismund; lower down are figures of Kings

Old Town Bridge Tower

33

Sculpture on the Charles Bridge: St Vitus and the Virgin with SS. Dominic and Thomas

Charles IV and Wenceslas IV, with St Vitus between them. The arch is decorated with the heraldic emblems of the territories ruled by the House of Luxemburg.

Lesser Quarter Bridge Towers

At the western end of the bridge are the Lesser Quarter Bridge Towers, linked by an arch. The lower tower (last quarter of 12th c.) formed part of the defences of the old Judith Bridge; the Renaissance pediment and the decoration of the outer walls were added in 1591. The other tower was built in 1464 at the behest of King George of Poděbrad. Its architecture and sculptural decoration are similar to those of the Old Town Bridge Tower.

*Charles Square (Karlovo náměstí)   C/D6/7

Location
Nové Město, Praha 1

Buses
120, 128, 137, 176

Trams
4, 14, 15, 16, 18, 19, 22, 24, 29

Charles Square is the largest square in Prague, measuring 530 m (580 yd) by 150 m (165 yd). Until 1848 the cattle market was held here. In its present form, with its lawns and trees and its statues of Czech scholars and writers, Charles Square is more like a park than a square.

On the south side of the square stands the Pharmacy of the Polyclinic, better known as the Faust House, on its east side the Church of St Ignatius, and at the north-east corner the tower of the former New Town Hall. In Resslova ulice, which leads from the west side of the square, are two other interesting churches, SS. Cyril and Methodius and St Wenceslas of Zderaz (see entries).

Faust House (Faustův dům)

The Faust House, originally a palace of the Late Renaissance, was altered during the construction of the town's fortifications between 1606 and 1617 and had a corner bastion built on to it. During the reign of Rudolf II (1575–1611) the English alchemist Edward Kelly carried out experiments here in the hope of producing gold. When another chemist installed his laboratory here in the 18th c. this gave rise to the legend that Dr Faust also occupied the house and, having sold his soul to the Devil, was carried off to Hell through the laboratory ceiling.

The Polyclinic thus seems to be following a well-established tradition in having its pharmacy here.

St Ignatius's Church (Kostel svatého Ignáce)

This Baroque church was built between 1665 and 1668 by Carlo Lurago, Architect to the Imperial Court, as the church of the former Jesuit college, which is now occupied by a section of the Polyclinic. The magnificent doorway (with a statue of St Ignatius in glory on the front pediment) was the work of Paul Ignaz Bayer.

The sumptuous interior has rich stucco ornament by A. Soldatti and altar-pieces by Karl Škréta and Ignaz Raab.

The Faust House in Charles Square

New Town Hall (Novoměstská radnice)

This building at the north-east corner of Charles Square, originally Gothic, was erected about 1347 as the Town Hall of the New Town. After the amalgamation of the Hradčany, the Lesser Quarter, the Old Town and the New Town and the transfer of municipal functions to the Old Town (1784), the New Town Hall was used as a prison, lawcourt and registry office. In the corner tower, built in 1452–56 and subsequently much altered and rebuilt, is a chapel.

The New Town was occupied mainly by the poorer classes of the population. The First Defenestration of Prague took place here on 13 June 1419, when a mob led by the preacher Jan Želivský stormed the New Town Hall, freed the Hussites confined in the prison and threw two Catholic councillors out of the window, giving the signal for the beginning of the Hussite Wars.

Charles University

See Carolinum

Clementinum (Klementinum)   C5(F/G10)

Location
Nám. primátora dr. V. Vacka
(Václav Vack Square), Staré
Město, Praha 1

Metro
Staroměstská

Buses
144, 156, 187

Tram
17

This former Jesuit college now houses the State Library of Czechoslovakia, with more than 5 million volumes, 6000 manuscripts (including the Codex Vyssegradensis) and more than 4000 incunabula.

After inheriting Bohemia and Hungary through his wife in 1526 Ferdinand I sought to re-Catholicise his hereditary territories without resorting to unduly harsh measures. In 1556 he summoned the Jesuits to Prague, and they took over the Monastery and Church of St Clement (see entry), which had been occupied by the Domincans since 1232. A whole quarter of the Old Town was pulled down to make room for the Clementinum, the largest complex of buildings in Prague after the Hradčany (see entry). In 1622 the Charles University (see Carolinum) was added to the complex.

The Clementinum includes within its area the churches of St Clement and St Salvator (see Knights of the Cross Square), a chapel belonging to the Italian community and an observatory (1751).

Notable features of the interior are the Library (known as the Baroque Hall) on the first floor, with ceiling-frescoes of the Muses; the Mozart Hall, with Rococo paintings; and the Mirror Chapel, now used for chamber concerts and exhibitions. There is an interesting collection of globes and table clocks in the Mathematical Hall.

In the south-west courtyard can be seen a statue of a Prague student, commemorating the occasion at the end of the Thirty Years War (1648) when the students defended the Charles Bridge against the Swedes.

Church of the Assumption and Charles the Great   D7
(Kostel Nanebevzetí Panny Marie a Karla Velikého)

This church, with an octagonal plan modelled on Charlemagne's Palatine Chapel in Aachen, was built by Charles IV in 1358. It was consecrated in 1377, still with a temporary roof. In 1575 Bonifaz Wohlmut completed the stellar vaulting, one of the most remarkable achievements of medieval architecture, with a span of 22·75 m (75 ft). It is accounted for by the old legend of the builder who sold his soul to the Devil in order to be able to complete his master work.

The church was remodelled in 1720 and subsequent years by Kilian Ignaz Dientzenhofer. The change in function from a monastic church to a place of pilgrimage and the addition of a number of chapels had the consequence of obscuring the original Gothic character of the church. Later the Baroque domes were added.

The Karlov Monastery, originally Gothic but remodelled in Baroque style by the Augustinian Canons in 1660–68, now houses the Museum of National Security and part of the State Archives.

Location
Nové Město, Praha 1

Metro
Gottwaldova, I. P. Pavlova

Trams
11, 19

Church of the Nativity

See Loreto

Cloth Hall (Dům Látek)   D5(G11)

The Cloth Hall, in the style of a Venetian Renaissance palazzo, was built in 1925–31 (architects, J. Zasch and P. Janák) for the Adria Insurance Company. It contains a piece of sculpture, "Adria", by Jan Štursa and other sculpture by Otto Gutfreund, Bohumil Kafka and K. Dvořák.

In the basement is the National Theatre's experimental theatre, the Laterna Magica (see Practical Information – Theatres).

Location
Národní 40, Nové Město, Praha 1

Metro
Můstek

Trams
5, 9, 29

Community House (Obecni dům)   D5(H10)

The Community House was built in 1906–11 (architects Antonín Balšanek and Osvald Polívka) on the site of an old royal stronghold established in 1380 and demolished in 1547.

Location
Náměstí republiky, Staré Město, Praha 1

Metro
Můstek

Trams
5, 9, 19, 29

Here on 28 October 1918 the Czech National Committee proclaimed the independance of the Czechoslovak Republic. This Jugendstil (Art Noveau) building, with a restaurant, a café, a wine-bar, exhibition halls and Prague's largest concert hall (the Smetana Hall), is a typical example of Czech Sezession architecture.

A whole generation of artists were involved in the external and internal decoration of the building. The Smetana Hall has sculpture by V. Novák and L. Saloun, the Primator's Hall paintings by Alfons Mucha, the Palacký Room a bust by J. V. Myslbek, etc.

Dvořák Museum

See Villa Amerika

Emmaus Abbey/Abbey of the Slavs   C7
(Emauzy/Klášter na Slovanech)

Location
Vyšehradská, Nové Město,
Praha 1

This former Benedictine abbey (dissolved in 1949) now houses a number of institutes of the Czechoslovak Academy of Sciences.

Emmaus Abbey

The abbey was founded by Charles IV in 1347, with Papal permission, for Benedictines of the Slav rite. Through this Order, reading the Mass in Old Slavonic, the Church sought to win over the eastern territories where the faith had made little headway.

In the 14th c. the abbey was an important centre of culture and education. The Glagolitic part of the Reims Gospel-Book, on which the kings of France swore their coronation oath, was preserved here until 1546. In 1945 the building was burnt out in an American air raid, and it has only recently been restored. The frescoes in the Gothic cloister (much restored) are among the finest work of the old Prague school of painting. In the manner of the late medieval "Biblia pauperum", they depict scenes from the Old and New Testaments in 26 panels. They are dated to about 1360.

St Mary's Church, now used mainly as a concert hall, was built between 1348 and 1372. Originally Gothic, with aisles of the same height as the nave, it was remodelled in Baroque style in the 17th c. and subsequently restored to neo-Gothic. The concave steeples of 1967 (architect F. M. Černý) represent a compromise between Baroque and Gothic.

Trams
18, 24

Ethnographic Museum (Národopisné muzeum) — B6

The Ethnographic Museum, a branch of the National Museum, occupies the old Villa Kinsky, set in the Kinsky Gardens to the south of the Hunger Wall (see Petřin Hill). The collection includes models of peasant houses, reproductions of rooms in typical houses, pottery, costumes, embroidery and much else of interest.

Behind the museum are a picturesque little bell-tower of Moravian-Wallachian type and a small 18th c. Ukrainian wooden church.

Location
Petřinské sady 98, Smíchov, Praha 5

Buses
176, 191

Opening times
Tues.–Sun. 10 a.m.–6 p.m.

---

*European Art Collection of the National Gallery — B4
(Sbírska evropského umění/Národní galerie)

From Hradčany Square (see entry) a street runs west past the Archbishop's Palace to the Sternberg (Šternberk) Palace, now occupied by the National Gallery's Collection of European Art. This High Baroque palace was designed by D. Martinelli and completed by J. B. Alliprandi in 1698–1707. It consists of four wings surrounding a courtyard, with a cylindrical projection. The walls of the courtyard have stucco ornament, and in the interior are ceiling-paintings by Pompeus Aldovrandini.

The collection includes works by painters of the Italian, Dutch and German schools (first and second floors) and by 19th and 20th c. painters from France and other European countries (upper floor and first floor). The rooms are not numbered but are arranged according to the artists' countries of origin.

The first floor is mainly devoted to painters of the Florentine school of the 14th and 15th c. (Sebastiano del Piombo, Orcagna, Giovanni d'Allemagna, Antonio Vivarini, Piero della Francesca, Palma il Vecchio, etc.).

The narrow room opening off the third room (on the left) contains icons from different countries.

Location
Hradčanské náměstí

Metro
Hradčanská

Trams
22, 23

Opening times
Tues.–Sun. 10 a.m.–6 p.m.

First floor

Dürer's "Festival of the Rosary"

Then follow Dutch and Flemish masters of the 15th and 16th c.: Geertgen tot Sint Jans, Gerard David, Jan Gossaert, known as Mabuse ("St Luke painting the Virgin"), Cornelis Engelbrechtsz, Pieter Brueghel the Elder ("Haymaking"), and Pieter Brueghel the Younger ("Winter Landscape", "Arrival of the Three Kings").

Second floor

The second floor begins with Italian painters of the 16th to 18th c., including works by Tintoretto ("David with Goliath's Head"), Veronese, Palma il Giovane, Bronzino, Tiepolo ("Portrait of a Venetian Patrician") and Canaletto ("View of London").

Then come German painters of the 14th to 18th c. The finest work here is Dürer's "Festival of the Rosary", painted in 1506 for German merchants in Venice. It shows the Virgin holding the Child and being crowned by angels, surrounded by numerous figures, including the artist himself (above, right), the humanist Konrad Peutinger, the wealthy German merchant Ulrich Fugger the Elder, the Emperor Maximilian I, Pope Julius II and a number of Venetians. There are also pictures by unknown 15th c. masters including the Master of Grossgmain and works by Hans of Tübingen, Hans Holbein the Elder, Hans Baldung Grien, Altdorfer, Lukas Cranach the Elder and Thomas Burgkmair.

There follow 17th c. Flemish and Dutch painters, including works by Jacob Jordaens ("Apostles"), Peter Paul Rubens ("Cleopatra", "Martyrdom of St Thomas" and "St Augustine on the Seashore", both 1637–39), David Teniers the Younger ("Boon Companions"), Antony van Dyck ("Abraham and Isaac"), Frans Hals ("Portrait of Jasper Schade van Westrum",

1645), Rembrandt ("Old Scholar", "Annunciation"), Adriaen van Ostade, Gerard Dou ("Young Woman on Balcony"), Metsu, Gerard Terborch (two portraits) and Philips Wouwerman.

The north and west wings are reached by keeping straight across the courtyard from the entrance.

North and West wings

French art of the 19th and 20th c., from the Romantic school to Cubism, arranged in chronological order according to the artists' dates of birth, with works by Delacroix, Daumier, Rousseau, Courbet, Monet, Cézanne, Renoir, Gauguin, van Gogh, Toulouse-Lautrec, Matisse, Vlaminck, Utrillo, Picasso (important paintings of the Early Cubist period), Braque and Chagall. Sculpture by Degas, Rodin, Bourdelle and Maillol.

Ground floor

On the first floor of the north and west wings is the collection of 19th and 20th c. European art, with works by Austrian (Ferdinand Georg Waldmüller, Gustav Klimt, Oskar Kokoschka), German (Casper David Friedrich, "The Bridge"), Russian (Ilya Repin) and Italian (Renato Guttuso; sculpture by Manzù) artists.

First floor

Faust House

See Charles Square

Federal National Assembly
(Areál budovy Federálního shromáždění ČSSR)

D6(H11)

The modern building which houses the Federal National Assembly of the Czechoslovak Socialist Republic was erected in 1967–72 as a symbol of the planned development along the north–south axis road. Equally symbolic is the piece of sculpture in front of the building, Vincenc Makovský's "New Era". The interior is decorated with works by modern artists. There are underpasses from the National Assembly to the Central Station and the Smetana Theatre (see Practical Information – Theatres).

Location
Vinohradská 1, Nové Město, Praha 1

Metro
Muzeum

Tram
11

Franciscan Garden (Františkánská zahrada)

See St Mary of the Snows

Grand Prior's Palace (Palác maltézského velkopřevora)

C5

The old Grand Prior's Palace of the Knights of Malta in the Lesser Quarter (see entry) is now occupied by the Music Department of the National Museum (Hudební oddelení Národního muzea), with a fine collection of musical instruments and a musical archive. Concerts are frequently given in the garden.

Location
Velkopřevorské nám. 4, Malá Strana, Praha 1

Trams
12, 22

Hibernian House

Opening times
Tues.–Sun. 10 a.m.–noon
and 1–5 p.m.

The palace, with two wings set at right angles, was built in
1726–31 by Bartolomeo Scotti, who remodelled an earlier
Renaissance building and added a new doorway, ornamental
cornices and oriel windows. The vases and statues holding
lamps are from the workshop of Matthias Braun.

Hibernian House (U hybernú)   D5(H10)

Location
Náměstí republiky
(Republic Square),
corner of Hybernská, Staré
Město, Praha 1

Metro Můstek

Trams
3, 5, 9, 10, 19, 26, 29

The exhibition and market hall known as U hybernú was
originally a Late Baroque church belonging to a friary of Irish
(Hiberian) Franciscans.
After the dissolution of the Franciscan Order J. Fischer
converted the church into a customs post with a neo-Classical
façade (1808–11). The sculptural decoration was the work of
F. X. Lederer (1811).
The building is also used for occasional cultural events.

High Synagogue

See Josefov

Holy Cross Chapel (Hradčany)

See Hradčany

Holy Cross Chapel (Old Town)   C5(F10/11)
(Rotunda svatého Kříže

Location
Ulice Karoliny Světlé,
corner of Konviktská, Staré
Město, Praha 1

Trams
5, 9, 17, 22

The Chapel of the Holy Cross, built about 1100, is one of only
three round chapels of the Romanesque period which survive
in Prague. A proposal during the 19th c. to pull it down was
frustrated by the opposition of the Czechs Artists' Union, and
instead of being demolished it was renovated by V. I. Ullmann
in 1865. The iron grille was the work of Josef Mánes. There are
remains of Gothic wall-painting in the interior of the chapel.

Holy Cross Church

See Na Příkopě

House signs

The dull and unimaginative method of identifying houses by
giving them numbers, following the French model, was
introduced in Prague as late as 1770, during the reign of Maria
Theresa. The use of house signs is much older. The use of family
names (surnames) became general in the 13th and 14th c., and
at the same time the practice was adopted of identifying houses
by names which were represented pictorially on the outside of

Some old Prague house signs

the building. At first the names usually referred to the situation of the house ("At the chestnut-tree", "At the bridge") or the owner's occupation ("At the salt-house", "At the mill"), but came to refer also to features related to religion ("At the sign of the Black Virgin", "At the sign of the Golden Angel"), to animals ("At the sign of the Stone Lamb", "At the sign of the Little Bears") or to heavenly bodies ("At the sign of the two Suns"). The house retained its name even if there was a change of ownership.

The house signs which visitors will come upon as they walk about Prague may be of stone, metal or wood, or sometimes of stucco or painted on plaster or tin; occasionally they may have an inscription.

The signs were so popular that they continued to be used even after the introduction of street-numbering in 1770, during the Empire and neo-Classical periods. Nowadays they are used mainly by restaurants and wine-houses.

There are so many houses with signs of this kind that they cannot possibly be listed here. They are mostly to be found in the old streets of the Lesser Quarter and the Old Town, but there are also some in Nerudova ulice, the picturesque street which leads to Hradčany Castle (see entry); No. 6, "At the sign of the Red Eagle"; No. 12, "At the sign of the Three Fiddles"; No. 16, "At the sign of the Golden Chalice".

**Hradčany (castle)   B4

Metro
Malostranská, Hradčanská

Tram
22

Opening times
Apr.–Oct., Tues.–Sun.
9 a.m.–5 p.m.;
Nov.–Mar., Tues.–Sun.
9 a.m.–4 p.m.

Conducted tours

Hradčany Castle has been the official residence of the President of the Republic since 1918.

Hradčany was founded by the Přemyslids at the end of the 9th c. as a timber-built stronghold surrounded by a mud wall. From 973 it was the residence not only of the ruling prince but of the bishop of the newly established diocese of Prague. In 1042, during the reign of Břetislav I, the castle was surrounded by a wall 2 m (6½ ft) thick and towers were built at the east and west ends; later a gateway was built on the south side. From 1135 onwards Soběslav I strengthened and developed the castle into a princely fortress in Romanesque style. The 30 m (100 ft) high Black Tower was used as a prison. In 1303 most of the structure was devastated by a fire. Work on the castle was resumed during the reign of Charles IV, in 1344. After the end of the Hussite Wars further alteration and rebuilding was carried out by the Jagellionian rulers and by Kings Vladislav (from 1471) and Louis (from 1516). During these building phases the first Renaissance features began to appear in

▼ *View of the Hradčany*

combination with the Late Gothic features. The Emperors Ferdinand I (from 1527) and Rudolf II (from 1575) enriched the castle and surrounding area with magnificent Renaissance buildings. In 1614 the Emperor Matthias built Prague's first secular Baroque structure, the gate at the west end. Originally a free-standing tower, this was incorporated in the outer wall of the first courtyard in the 18th c. at the behest of Maria Theresa.

This building phase gave the Hradčany the architectural unity which makes it the dominant feature of the city's skyline to this day. After the declaration of the Republic in 1918 and the liberation of 1945 it was used for major State and public occasions and ceremonies.

In order to get an idea of the scale of the Hradčany and the multiplicity of buildings it contains, the best plan is to begin by walking round the various courtyards or outer wards with their little streets and lanes and then to visit the individual buildings.

Outer wards

The first and most recent of the courtyards, also known as the Grand Courtyard, is entered from Hradčany Square (Hradčanské náměstí; see entry) through a wrought-iron gateway flanked by piers bearing copies of Ignaz Platzer the Elder's "Fighting Giants" (1786).

First Courtyard
(První nádoří)

The First Courtyard was created in the reign of Maria Theresa, between 1756 and 1774; the plans were prepared in Vienna by the Court Architect, Nikolaus Pacassi, and the work was directed by Anselmo Lurago. The sculptured trophies on the attics of the building are originals by Platzer. The most recent alterations to the courtyard were carried out by the Slovene architect Josip Plečnik in 1920–22.

The gate which bears the Emperor Matthias's name was built for him by Giovanni Maria Philippi in 1614 as a free-standing western entrance to the Hradčany. In 1760 the gate-tower was

Matthias Gate
(Matyasova brána)

linked with the newly built front wall of the castle by N. Pacassi. From the gate a flight of steps (by Pacassi, 1765–66) leads up to the State apartments of the castle – the Throne Room, a room containing paintings by Václav Brožik, the Hall of Mirrors, the Music Room and the Drawing Room. This range of buildings also contains the private apartments of the President of the Republic.

The flagpoles outside the Matthias Gate are firs from the forests on the frontiers of Czechoslovakia – an idea conceived by the architect, J. Plečnik.

Second Courtyard
(Druhé nádvoří)

The Matthias Gate leads into the Second Courtyard, in the centre of which is a Baroque well-house, built by Francesco della Torre in 1686, with sculpture by Hieronymus Kohl. The wrought-iron grille dates from 1702.

The austerity of this courtyard is relieved by the modern Lion Fountain (V. Makovský, 1967) and the gleaming granite paving (J. Frágner, also 1967).

On the north side of the courtyard is the Plečnik Hall, created in 1927–31 by the reconstruction of older buildings, which was combined with the so-called Staircase Hall to form an entrance lobby to the Spanish Hall and the Rodulf Gallery.

From the Second Court a bridge (the Dusty Bridge; Prasný most) leads over the Deer-Pit; then, passing through St Mary's Work (Mariánské hradby) and continuing past the Royal Garden (open only in spring) and the old Ballroom, we come to Belvedere Palace (see entry).

Third Courtyard
(Tretí nádvoří)

The Third Courtyard was the centre of the castle's life. This was the starting-point of the main street of the old Slav settlement. On the north side of the courtyard is St Vitus's Cathedral. Under the south wall of the cathedral can be seen the foundations (excavated 1920–28) of a Romanesque episcopal chapel. Between 1750 and 1770 the older buildings of the royal stronghold were given a uniform façade by N. Pacassi (Rudolf II's Renaissance palace, the Early Baroque Queen's Palace and the Palace of Maximilian II). Under the balcony with statues holding lamps (by Ignaz Platzer) is the entrance to the offices of the President of the Republic.

Golden Lane
(Zlatá ulička)

The Golden Lane (also called the Gold-Makers' Lane) runs between the castle walls built by Vladislav Jagiello and the Old Castellan's Lodging. Originally it continued to St George's Convent. Along its north side ran the wall-walk between the Daliborka Tower and the White Tower. The north side of the street has been preserved, with its tiny picturesque houses built into the arches under the wall-walk. Rudolf II assigned these houses to the 24 members of his castle guard, who followed various trades in their leisure time. The name of Gold-Makers' Street or Alchemists' Street refers to Rudolf II's alchemists, who are traditionally said to have lived and sought to produce gold in these houses. It is known, however, that their laboratories were in the Mihulkar Tower. The houses were later occupied by craftsmen and the poorer members of the community. In 1912–14 Franz Kafka lived and wrote here. The houses are now occupied by small shops (souvenirs, etc.).

South-east end of castle precincts

The former Castellan's Lodging is now the House of Czechoslovak Children. Going past the Daliborka Tower and Black Tower, we can continue over the Bastion (view) and down the Old Castle Steps into the lane called Pod Bruskou.

Entrance to the First Courtyard of the Hradčany

Golden Lane, the street of the alchemists

To the west of the Bastion is the Rampart Garden (views). Two obelisks mark the spots where the Emperor's representatives fell when thrown out of the window in the Second Defenstration of Prague. Above the New Castle Steps is the Paradise Garden, with the Matthias Pavilion.

*Castle Gallery (Hradní galerie)

The Castle Gallery was created in 1965 by converting the old court stables in the north wing and the ground floor of the west wing. Its six rooms contain a total of 70 pictures from the old Rudolf Gallery and the Castle Gallery established by Ferdinand II and later broken up. Among the most notable works are a portrait of the Emperor Matthias painted by Hans of Aachen about 1612, Titian's "Young Woman at her Toilet", Tintoretto's "Woman taken in Adultery", Veronese's "St Catherine with Angel" and Rubens's "Assembly of the Olympian Gods" (*c.* 1602). The collection also includes pictures by Bohemian

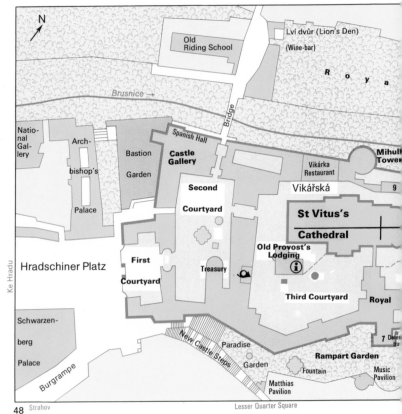

artists of the Baroque period (Jan Kupecký. Johann Peter Brand) and sculpture by Adriaen de Vries ("Adoration of the Kings") and Matthias Braun.

Chapel of the Holy Cross (Kaple svatého Kříže)

At the south corner of the Second Courtyard is the Chapel of the Holy Cross, which since 1961 has housed the Treasury of St Vitus's Cathedral. It contains valuable liturgical utensils, vestments, monstrances and reliquaries, St Wenceslas's coat of mail, St Stephen's sword and other relics.
The chapel was built in 1753 by Anselmo Lurago, but was altered between 1852 and 1858, during the Biedermeier period, with the idea of relieving its neo-Classical severity. The statue of St John of Nepomuk in the interior and those of SS. Peter and Paul in niches are by E. Max (1854). The sculpture of the high and side altars is by Ignaz Platzer. The chapel also contains paintings by W. Kandler, J. Navrátil and F. X. Palko.

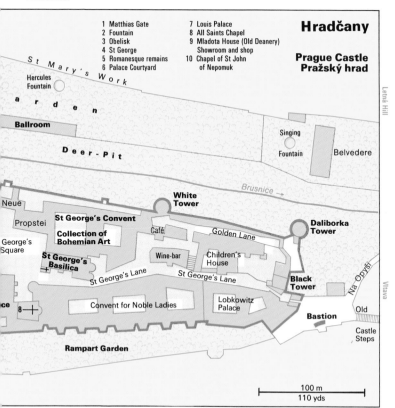

1 Matthias Gate
2 Fountain
3 Obelisk
4 St George
5 Romanesque remains
6 Palace Courtyard
7 Louis Palace
8 All Saints Chapel
9 Mladota House (Old Deanery) Showroom and shop
10 Chapel of St John of Nepomuk

Hradčany

Prague Castle
Pražský hrad

St Mary's Work

Hercules Fountain

Garden

Ballroom

Deer-Pit

Singing Fountain

Belvedere

Letná Hill

Brusnice →

Neue

White Tower

Propstei

St George's Convent

Café

Golden Lane

Daliborka Tower

Collection of Bohemian Art

George's Square

St George's Basilica

Wine-bar

Children's House

St George's Lane

St George's Lane

Black Tower

Na Opyši

Vltava

Convent for Noble Ladies

Lobkowicz Palace

Bastion

Old Castle Steps

Rampart Garden

ce 8

100 m
110 yds

Old Provost's Lodging (Staré proboštsví)

At the south-west corner of St Vitus's Cathedral is the Old Provost's Lodging. Originally a Romanesque episcopal palace, it was given its present Baroque form in the 17th c. The statue of St Wenceslas is by Johann Georg Bendl (1662).

On the south side of the Old Provost's Lodging stands an obelisk of Mrákotin granite (by J. Plečnik, 1928) commemorating the dead of the First World War.

The equestrian statue of St George (a copy: the original is in St George's Convent), in Early Gothic style, was the work of Georg and Martin of Cluj (1373); it was restored by Tomáš Jaros after a fire in 1541. The present base is by J. Plečnik (1928).

* * St Vitus's Cathedral (Chrám svatého Víta)

St Vitus's Cathedral, the metropolitan church of the archdiocese of Prague, stands on the site of a round chapel which Duke (St) Wenceslas dedicated to St Vitus in 925.

A hundred years later Duke Spytihněv II founded a Romanesque basilican church with a double choir. In 1344 Charles IV began the construction of the present Gothic cathedral.

The east end was designed by the French architect Matthias of Arras, following the older French Gothic style (Narbonne and Toulouse Cathedrals). He was responsible for the choir (47 m (154 ft) long, 39 m (128 ft) high), though only the lower part of it was completed when he died in 1352. His successor, Peter Parler, enriched the structure with the upward-soaring German Gothic forms. The work was continued by his sons Wenzel and Johann (1399–1420), who completed the choir with its ring of chapels and built the lower part of the main tower. After the Hussite Wars Bonifaz Wohlmut topped the tower with a Renaissance steeple and balustrade, bringing it to a total height of 109 m (358 ft); and finally, in 1770, it was given its onion dome by N. Pacassi.

The neo-Gothic western part of the cathedral was built by Josef Mocker and Kamil Hilbert from 1872 onwards. The west end was completed only in 1929.

St Vitus's Cathedral is not only Prague's most imposing church and the finest building in the Hradčany: it is also the city's largest church, with a total length of 124 m (407 ft), a breadth of 60 m (197 ft) across the transepts and a height of 33 m (108 ft) in the nave. In the south tower – an unusual combination of Gothic, Baroque and Renaissance elements – are three Renaissance bells and the largest church bell in Bohemia, the bronze Sigismund Bell (1549).

Interior

South doorway. The cathedral is best entered by the south doorway. On the upper part of this sumptuous portal, known as the Golden Gate (Zlatá brána), are portraits of Charles IV and Elisabeth of Pomerania and a much-restored 14th c. mosaic of the Last Judgement. Above this is a traceried window by Max Svabinský (1934), also representing the Last Judgement, which contains no fewer than 40,000 separate pieces of glass.

St Vitus's Cathedral ▶

Triforium gallery. The best plan is to leave the side chapels for the moment and get a general impression of this massive building with its 28 piers and 21 chapels, from the centre of the cathedral.

The triforium gallery runs above the arcading and below the windows of the choir. Within the triforium, and particularly over the organ gallery, are busts of the cathedral architects, Charles IV's family and other notable personages. These busts, mostly from the Parlers' workshop, formed the first gallery of portraits of historical figures in Europe before the Renaissance. There is no access to the triforium, but there are casts of the busts in the Royal Palace (see p. 58) and in Karlštejn Castle (see entry).

Organ gallery. The two-storey organ gallery (by Bonifaz Wohlmut, 1557–61) is opposite the south doorway. After the completion of the cathedral it was moved from its original position at the west end to the north aisle. The organ (1757) has 6500 pipes.

Imperial Mausoleum. In the centre of the choir, in front of the high altar, is the white marble Imperial Mausoleum, surrounded by a Renaissance screen (by J. Schmidthammer, 1589). The mausoleum was begun in Innsbruck in 1564 as a memorial to Ferdinand I and his wife Anna Jagiello and remodelled in the reign of Rudolf II (completed 1589). The figures on the cover are Anna Jagiello, Ferdinand I (centre) and Maximilian II. In medallions along the sides are representations of the kings and queens of Bohemia who are buried in the vault under the mausoleum.

St Vitus's Cathedral: the nave (left) and one of the fine stained-glass windows

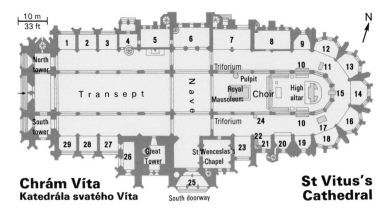

Chrám Víta
Katedrála svatého Víta

South doorway

St Vitus's
Cathedral

1 Bartoň-Dobenín Chapel
2 Schwarzenberg Chapel
3 New Archbishops' Chapel (Hora Chapel)
4 Old Treasury
5 New Sacristy
6 Wohlmut's choir (organ gallery)
7 St Sigismund's Chapel (Czernin Chapel)
8 Old Sacristy (formerly St Michael's Chapel)
9 St Anne's Chapel (Nostitz Chapel)
10 Historical reliefs
11 Statue of Cardinal von Schwarzenberg
12 Old Archbishops' Chapel
13 Chapel of John the Baptist (Pernstein Chapel)
14 Lady Chapel (Trinity Chapel, Imperial Chapel)
15 Tomb of St Vitus
16 Reliquary Chapel (Saxon Chapel, Sternberg Chapel)
17 Tomb of St John of Nepomuk
18 Chapel of St John of Nepomuk (St Adalbert's Chapel)
19 Waldstein Chapel (Magdalene Chapel)
20 Vladislav Oratory (Royal Oratory)
21 Holy Cross Chapel
22 Entrance to Royal Vault
23 St Andrew's Chapel (Martinitz Chapel)
24 Monument of Count Schlick
25 Crown Rooms
26 Chapter Library
27 Thun Chapel
28 Chapel of Holy Sepulchre
29 St Ludmilla's Chapel (Baptistery)

Burial vault. The entrance to the vault is beside the Holy Cross Chapel. In the passages archaeological finds of the Romanesque period are displayed. On the wall is a ground-plan of the old Romanesque church.

The sarcophagi in the upper tier are those of George of Poděbrad (1420–71: left), Charles IV (1316–78: centre) and Ladislav Postumus (1440–57: right). In the lower tier are Wenceslas IV (1361–1419), his brother John of Görlitz (d. 1396) and the common sarcophagus of Charles IV's four wives. To the rear is Maria Amalia, Maria Theresa's daughter. A Renaissance sarcophagus in pewter contains the remains of Rudolf II (1552–1612), and a low granite sarcophagus those of Charles IV's children.

Old Sacristy. Visitors leave the burial vault by a staircase which emerges in front of the choir screen. To the left is the Old Sacristy, which formerly contained the cathedral treasury (now in the Holy Cross Chapel in the Second Courtyard). Note the fine stellar vaulting.

St Anne's Chapel. Immediately east of the Old Sacristy is St Anne's Chapel, opposite which is the first part of a relief wood-carving attributed to Caspar Bechterle of Niedersonthofen depicting the destruction of images in the cathedral in 1619; its

53

St Vitus's Cathedral: the Bishop's throne

counterpart on the south side of the ambulatory depicts the flight of the "Winter King", Frederick V of the Palatinate, after the Battle of the White Mountain. Also of interest is a view of Prague as it was at that period (drawn about 1630).

Just beyond St Anne's Chapel is a kneeling figure, in bronze, of Cardinal Friedrich von Schwarzenberg (d. 1885) by Josef Václav Myslbek (1904).

Archbishops' Chapel. Opposite the Schwarzenberg statue is the Archbishops' Chapel, with the burial vault of the archbishops of Prague.

Chapel of John the Baptist. This adjoins the Archbishops' Chapel. To the right and left are the tombs of Břetislav II (d. 1100) and Bořivoj II (d. 1124). The bronze candelabra to the left of the altar is said to have come from Vladislav II's share of the booty brought back by Frederick Barbarossa from Milan. The Romanesque base of the candelabra came from the Rhineland.

Lady Chapel. In the Lady Chapel are the tombs of Břetislav I (1034–55) and Spytihněv II (1055–61), both from the Parlers' workshop. Opposite the chapel, behind the high altar, can be seen the Tomb of St Vitus, with a statue of the Saint by Josef Max.

Reliquary Chapel. This chapel, also known as the Saxon Chapel, contains the tombs of Přemysl Ottokar I (1192–93 and 1198–1230), on the right, and Přemysl Ottokar II (1253–78), on the left. Both are from the Parlers' workshop.

Chapel of St John of Nepomuk, next to the Reliquary Chapel; also known as St Adalbert's Chapel. On the altar are silver busts of SS. Adalbert, Wenceslas, Vitus and Cyril (c. 1699).

Opposite the chapel is the sumptuous silver Tomb of St John of Nepomuk, made in Vienna in 1733–36 to the design of Joseph Emanuel Fischer von Erlach.

Opposite the next chapel, the Waldstein or Magdalene Chapel (with the Waldstein family vault), is the second part of the relief by Caspar Bechterle (above, p. 53).

Royal or Vladislav Oratory. This chapel is now attributed to a Frankfurt sculptor named Hans Spiess. It is a richly decorated Late Gothic structure with a naturalistic pattern of interwoven branches on the front, formed of two intersecting arches with a pendant boss.

Chapel of the Holy Cross. On the left-hand wall of this chapel is a painting of the Vernicle (1369), with representations of the six patron saints of Bohemia on the frame. Entrance to the Royal Burial Vault.

St Andrew's Chapel. In this chapel, also known as the Martinitz Chapel, is the gravestone (to the left, under the window) of Jaroslav von Martinitz (d. 1649), one of the two victims of the Second Defenestration of Prague.

Monument of Count Schlick. On the first pier opposite St Wenceslas's Chapel is the Baroque monument of Field-Marshal Count Schlick (d. 1723), by Matthias Braun (to the design of J. E. Fischer von Erlach).

St Wenceslas's Chapel. The finest of the choir chapels is the Gothic Chapel of St Wenceslas, which extends into the south transept. It was built by Peter Parler in 1358–67, replacing the original round chapel of the Romanesque period in which the Saint was buried. It contains the Shrine of St Wencelsas, Duke of Bohemia, who was murdered by his brother Boleslav in 929 or 935. The lion's-head door-ring to which he clung when attacked by Boleslav is preserved here.

The lower part of the walls of the chapel is decorated with 1300 Bohemian semi-precious stones. The lower register of wall-paintings (the Passion cycle) is by Master Oswald of Prague (1373); the upper register (legend of St Wencelsas) is from the studio of the Master of the Litoměřice Altar (c. 1509). The polychrome painting of the statue of St Wenceslas on the east wall between two angels (Heinrich Parler, 1373) is by Master Oswald. The bronze candelabra at the left-hand end of the wall was the work of Hans Vischer of Nuremberg (1532).

Crown Rooms. From St Wenceslas's Chapel a staircase leads up to the Crown Rooms over the south doorway in which the Bohemian Crown Jewels and insignia are kept. They are open to the public only at certain specified times.

Royal Palace (Královský palác)

The Royal Palace, the history of which down the centuries is reflected in its architecture, is in the Third Courtyard. It was the

Two of the finest rooms in the royal palace: Vladislav Hall . . .

. . . and the Hall of the Diet

royal residence until the end of the 16th c., but when, under the Habsburgs, the royal residence moved west it was used as offices and store-rooms.

Part of the original Romanesque palace has survived in the ground and basement floors below the present Vladislav Hall. The remains of the original palace were concealed under new building by Přemysl Ottokar II, Charles IV and Wenceslas IV, and later Vladislav Jagiello built or rebuilt a new floor, in the centre of which is the Vladislav Hall, the most splendid of the secular buildings in the Hradčany.

The entrances to the palace are on the east side of the Third Courtyard.

Green Room. The central doorway under the balcony, to the right of the Eagle Fountain (by Francesco Torre, 1664), leads into an antechamber, with the Green Room to the left. From the time of Charles IV this was used as a court room. The ceiling-fresco of the Judgement of Solomon (copy) was installed here in 1960. The Green Room gives access to Vladislav's Bedroom and the Map Repository.

Vladislav Hall (Vladislavský sál). The Vladislav Hall, also known as the Hall of Homage, was built by Benedikt Ried between 1493 and 1503. With its considerable dimensions (62 m (203 ft) long, 16 m (52 ft) wide, 13 m (43 ft) high) and its beautiful Late Gothic reticulated vaulting it is one of the show-pieces of the Hradčany. In this hall the Bohemian kings were elected, and it has been used since 1934 for the election of the President of the Republic.

Hall of the Diet. The doorway at the north-east corner of the Vladislav Hall leads into the Hall of the Diet, also built by Benedikt Ried (c. 1500). After being devastated by fire it was

**Royal Palace
Královský palác**

1 Eagle Fountain	5 Romanesque tower	9 All Saints Chapel
2 Antechamber	6 Bohemian Chancellery	10 Hall of Diet
3 Green Room	7 Theresian range	11 Staircase (for horsemen)
4 Vladislav's Bedroom	8 Outlook terrace	12 New Appeal Court

rebuilt in 1559–63 by Bonifaz Wohlmut with ribbed vaulting in imitation of Late Gothic architecture.

The rostrum for the Clerk to the Diet is Renaissance. On the walls are portraits of Habsburg rulers.

New Map Room. The entrance to this room, which dates in its present form from the 17th c., is to the left of the doorway into the Hall of the Diet. On the walls are the coats of arms of officials of the Map Repository.

Staircase. This is no ordinary staircase but one specially designed for horsemen, who could thus ride up into the Vladislav Hall for the tournaments which were held there.

Palace Courtyard. A doorway on the right at the foot of the staircase leads into St George's Square, the one on the left into the Palace Courtyard, surrounded on two sides by arcades. Another staircase gives access to the Gothic Palace (not at present open to the public).

Other features of the palace: Old Map Room, with massive vaulting borne on two squat piers; an arcaded passage from the time of Přemysl Ottokar II; the Charles Room, with casts of the Parler busts in the triforium of St Vitus's Cathedral; the Old Registry (or Palace Kitchen); and Wenceslas IV's Columned Hall, with late 15th c. Gothic vaulting.

Basement. A steep staircase leads down from the Palace Courtyard to the basement of the palace, in which visitors can see remains of early castle walls, some dating from the 9th c. (The basement and the adjoining Soběslav Palace, of the Romanesque period, are not at present open to the public.)

Louis Palace

The Louis Palace which adjoins the Vladislav Hall was built by Benedikt Ried between 1502 and 1509 for Vladislav II. It contains the apartments occupied by the Bohemian Chancellery. The larger room with Gothic vaulting was the seat of the Governor of Bohemia. The smaller Council Chamber is entered from this room through a Renaissance doorway.

From the windows of the room in the tower, on 23 May 1618, the Emperor's Deputy Governors Jaroslav von Martinitz and Wilhelm Slavata, together with their clerk Fabricius, were thrown 15 m (50 ft) down into the castle moat (but, according to a contemporary account, "got off with the fear of death, their lives and a few scratches"). This Second Defenestration of Prague gave the signal for the Bohemian rising against the Habsburgs and led to the Thirty Years War.

From here a spiral staircase leads to the former Chancellery (Late Renaissance) of the Imperial Council.

Another spiral staircase (not at present open) leads back to the Vladislav Hall.

All Saints Chapel. A short flight of steps at the east end of the Vladislav Hall gives access to the All Saints Chapel (by Peter Parler, 1370–87). Notable features are the cycle of paintings by Christian Dittmann on the lives of saints (1669), V. V. Reiner's All Saints altar-piece (1732) and Hans of Aachen's Angels triptych.

The chapel originally belonged to the convent for noble ladies which adjoined the palace on the east.

St George's Basilica

St George's Basilica (Bazilika svatého Jiří)

At the east end of St George's Square, facing the chancel of St Vitus's Cathedral, is the twin-towered Romanesque Basilica of St George, the oldest surviving church in the Hradčany, which is now used as a concert hall.

The church was founded by Duke Vratislav I in 912 and consecrated about 925. It was devastated by fire in 1142 and again in 1541, and was much altered and rebuilt in the course of its history. The present Baroque façade dates from about 1670.

During renovation work in 1897–1907 and 1959–62 the original Romanesque character of the church was restored: the exterior marked by its slender white towers, the interior by the alternation of pillars and columns and the triple-arched galleries in the thick walls over the arcading.

South doorway

The south doorway (*c.* 1500), in Early Renaissance style, came from the workshop of Benedikt Ried; it is decorated with a copy of a Late Gothic relief of St George. St Ludmilla's Chapel, built on by Peter Parler about 1380, contains the Tomb of St Ludmilla (murdered in 921), one of Bohemia's patron saints.

Choir and crypt

The raised choir has remains of Romanesque ceiling-paintings ("Heavenly Jerusalem", after 1200). In front of the entrance to the crypt is the monument of Duke Boleslav II (d. 999), enclosed within wrought-iron Baroque screens. To the right is the painted wooden tomb of Vratislav I (d. 921).

Chapel of St John of Nepomuk
Built on to the south wall of the church is the Chapel of St John of Nepomuk (by F. M. Kaňka, 1718–22). The statue of the Saint on the façade is by Ferdinand Maximilian Brokoff. Notable features of the interior are the frescoes in the dome and the altar-piece by V. V. Reiner.

Collection of Old Bohemian Art of the National Gallery
(Sbírka starého českého umění/Národní galerie)

Adjoining St George's Basilica stands the Benedictine Convent of St George, a nunnery founded in 973 by Duke Boleslav II and his sister Mlada. This pre-Romanesque (Ottonian) building is the oldest religious house in Bohemia. After being damaged by fire in 1142 and again in 1541 it was much altered, enlarged and remodelled in Baroque style (1657–80). It was dissolved in 1782, and now houses the National Gallery's collection of old Bohemian art.

Lower floor

The collection is arranged chronologically, beginning with Gothic on the lower floor. The sculpture and panel-paintings are mostly from churches in Bohemia. The artists, whose names are unknown, are identified by reference to their works and to the places where they were found. The commonest theme in medieval Bohemian art is the Virgin.

St George's Convent

Collection of Old Bohemian Art

St George's Basilica

3

2

1

4

10 m
33 ft

1 Tombs of Přemyslid rulers
2 St Ludmilla's Chapel
3 Chapel of St John of Nepomuk
4 St Anne's Chapel

St George's Basilica and Covent

Bazilika a klášter svatého Jiří

Thanks to the munificent patronage of Charles IV Gothic art flourished in Bohemia, and continued to thrive after his reign – for example in the Prague school of painters, represented here by their finest works.

North corridor
The long north corridor is dominated by the monumental tympanum from the Church of St Mary of the Snows (see entry; 1346) and Early Gothic Madonnas.

Cycle of the Master of Hohenfurth (Vyši Brod)
A separate room is devoted to the Cycle of the Master of Hohenfurth (Mistr vyšebrodského oltáře), an altar-piece of nine panels (c. 1330–50) from the Cistercian house of Hohenfurth (now Vyši Brod): Annunciation, Nativity, Adoration of the Kings, Resurrection.

Equestrian statue of St George
Farther along the north corridor is the original of the statue of St George in the Third Courtyard. This bronze figure, cast by Martin and George of Cluj (Klausenburg) in 1373, is the earliest free-standing piece of sculpture north of the Alps.

Room of Master Theoderich
This room adjoins the north corridor. Theoderich, the only painter represented here whose name is known, is a representative of the style known to German art scholars as the "beautiful" or "soft" style of Gothic painting in Bohemia. He painted 128 panel-paintings for Charles IV in Karlštejn Castle (see entry), six of which can be seen here. The votive picture of Archbishop John Očko of Vlašim (c. 1370) and the "Crucifixion" from Emmaus Abbey (see entry) reach out beyond the "soft" style.

Corridor
The long corridor displays fine statues of the late 14th c. Smaller items are shown in cases.

Cycle of the Master of Wittingau   Ground floor
The first room on the ground floor is devoted to the Cycle of the Master of Wittingau (Mistr třeboňského oltáře), of which there are only fragmentary remains. The three panels depict: on the front Christ on the Mount of Olives, the Resurrection and the Entombment; on the back a cycle of saints, also from the workshop of the Master of Wittingau (who himself painted only the heads).

Tympanum from the Týn Church
A room opening off the north corridor displays the tympanum from the north doorway of the Týn Church (see entry; Peter Parler's workshop, 1402–10), with three scenes from the Passion cycle – the Scourging, Calvary and the Crowning with Thorns.

North corridor
The north corridor contains paintings and sculpture illustrating the development of Late Gothic art in Bohemia, with special reference to the "soft" style. Notable among the representations of the Virgin are the Madonna suckling the Infant Christ from Konopiště (c. 1380), the Madonna of Český Krulov (c. 1400) and the Madonna of Zlatá Koruna (1410).

The Crucifixion by the Master of Raigern (early 15th c.), with its almost caricatural distortion of the figures, marks a turning-point in Bohemian painting.

Renaissance works
Notable among the Renaissance works in the collection are the "Visitation" (1505) by the Master of Leitmeritz (Litoměřice), the "Lamentation" from Zebrák and the carved wood altar shrine by Master IP (known only by his initials; c. 1520), which is in the last room before the stairs up to the first floor.

First floor

The works on the first floor show the development from Mannerism (end of 16th c.) through Baroque and Rococo to the end of the 18th c.

Mannerism
At the beginning of this section are the artists belonging to the northern school of Mannerism at the Court of Rudolf II (1575–1612): the painters Bartholomäus Spranger, Hans of Aachen, Josef Heinz and Roelandt Savery and the sculptor Adriaen de Vries.

Baroque
Painting: Karel Škréta, Peter Brandl, Johannes Kupetzky (a room of his own), V. V. Reiner, Michael Leopold Willmann, Johannes Christoph Lischka. Sculpture: important works by Ignaz Franz Platzer, Matthias Bernhard Braun and Johann Georg Bendl.

Rococo
The development from Baroque to Rococo is seen in pictures by Anton Kern and Norbert Grund.

---

*Hradčany Square (Hradčanské náměstí)   B4

Location
Hradčany, Praha 1

Metro
Hradčanská

Trams
22, 23

The little town of Hradčany was founded about 1320, the third settlement on the site of Prague. It did not enjoy independent municipal status, subject only to the Crown, but owed allegiance to the Castellan of the castle on Hradčany Hill. Originally it covered only the area of the present Hradčany Square, but in the reign of Charles IV it was extended towards the north and surrounded by walls.

Hradčany Square, with its Baroque Plague Column (by F. M. Brokoff, 1725), forms the approach to Prague Castle (see Hradčany), and lay on the processional route followed at the coronation of the kings of Bohemia. Here in 1547 the leaders of the abortive rising against the Habsburg King Ferdinand I were executed. Although it has the scale and layout of a medieval market-place it never performed this function.

After the city fire in 1541 the square was completely rebuilt, all the old burghers' houses being pulled down to make way for palaces.

Archbishop's Palace, Hradčany Square

Archbishop's Palace (Arcibiskupský palác)

The Archbishop's Palace on the north side of the square was originally a Renaissance mansion which Ferdinand I bought from the royal Private Secretary Florian von Gryspek and presented to the first post-Hussite Catholic Archbishop of Prague. It was rebuilt in 1562–64 and remodelled in Baroque style, with a magnificent new doorway, by the French architect Jean-Baptiste Mathey in 1669. It was given its present Rococo form, with marble facing on the façade, by Johann Joseph Wirch (1763–64), who was also responsible for the sumptuous interior decoration.

Opening times
Only on Maundy Thursday
9 a.m.–5 p.m.

Martinitz Palace

At the north-west corner of the square is the Martinitz Palace. This handsome Renaissance palace was originally built for Andreas Teyfl at the end of the 16th c. as a plain building of four wings set round a courtyard. In 1624 it was acquired by Jaroslav Borita von Martinitz, known to history as one of the two Imperial councillors who suffered defenestration in 1618. He added an extra storey, together with the Renaissance gables and coats of arms. The east front has figural sgraffito decoration depicting scenes from the life of Samson (after 15th c. German woodcuts) and the life of Hercules (*c.* 1634). During recent restoration work similar sgraffito decoration depicting Biblical scenes was discovered on the side facing the square.

Schwarzenberg Palace and Museum of Military History
(Schwarzenberg-palota, Vojenské muzeum)

Opening times
May–Oct., Tues.–Sun.
9 a.m.–3.30 p.m.

The Schwarzenberg Palace, which now houses the Swiss Embassy as well as the Museum of Military History, ranks with the Castle and the Archbishop's Palace as a dominant feature in the panorama of the Hradčany. With its richly decorated gables, its sgraffito ornamentation in imitation of faceted masonry and its representations of Classical divinities and allegorical figures, it is a very characteristic example of the Renaissance architecture of northern Europe.

The palace, on the south side of the square, was created in 1800–10 by the reconstruction in Empire style for Archbishop Salm – hence the initial S over the doorway – of two Renaissance mansions; the architect was F. Paviček.

The Museum is in the right-hand part of the building (1545–63, by Agostino Galli). It illustrates the development of the art of war down to 1918, with examples of prehistoric weapons and the great variety of armaments used by European armies over the centuries. The courtyard contains cannon and naval guns of the 16th to 20th c. There are also extensive displays of army uniforms of all ranks and many different countries, a collection of medals, flags and banners, maps and plans of important battles.

Jewish Town Hall

See Josefov

* * Josefov (Joseph's Town, Jews' Town)   C/D4(G9)

Location
Jáchymova,
Staré Město, Praha 1

Metro
Staroměstská

Buses
133, 144, 156, 197

Tram
17

In the northern part of the Old Town is the old Jewish quarter which came to be known as Joseph's Town. A number of buildings in this quarter, including the Town Hall, the Synagogues and the cemetery, are open to the public as part of the State Jewish Museum.

History

The Jews were probably already settled in Prague before the 10th c., and by the 13th c. lived in a separate quarter enclosed by a wall, following the decision of the Third Lateran Council (1179) that the Jews should be separated from the dwellings of the Christians by a fence, a wall or a moat. This ghetto was considerably extended in the 17th c. In the reigns of the Habsburg rulers Maximilian and Rudolf II there were at times more than 7000 Jews crowded into an area of increasingly cramped and sunless lanes.

Rudolf II's Minister of Finance, Mordechaj Markus Maisl, had the streets of the ghetto paved, built the Jewish Town Hall and Maisl Synagogue and established the Old Jewish Cemetery which now attracts so many visitors.

In 1512 the first Hebrew printing-press in Central Europe was set up in this quarter. Schools, synagogues and public baths, an infirmary, a poor-house and a burial fraternity were established. A notable inhabitant of the ghetto (1573 onwards) was Rabbi Löw, a theologian and student of the

Cabbala who features in many legends and is said to have created a golem (an artificial human being). The Jewish quarter, however, was frequently ravaged by fires (1378, 1754) and by pogroms.

The Empress Maria Theresa (1743–80) abolished the requirement that Jews should live in the ghetto, and Joseph II (1780–90) made the old Jews' Town the fifth ward of the town of Prague. Thereafter it became known as Joseph's Town (Josefov).

The freedom of residence granted to the Jews led to considerable changes in the population structure of Joseph's Town. From the outside the houses looked picturesque, but they were dilapidated and had no water-supply or drainage. Until 1893 this was the poor quarter of Prague.

The slum clearance which began in 1893 left only the buildings of historical interest still standing, and these now form the State Jewish Museum.

Until 1939 many of Prague's Jews were German-speaking, and writers such as Franz Kafka, Franz Werfel, Egon Erwin Kisch and Max Brod made a major contribution to German literature in the years between the two world wars. The Nazi occupation of 1939–45, however, dealt a mortal blow to the city's lively Jewish community. During the Second World War 90 per cent of the Jewish population of Bohemia and Moravia were killed: their names are inscribed on the "Memorial of the 77,297" set up in the Pinkas Synagogue to commemorate the victims of the Nazi terror.

State Jewish Museum (Státní Židovské muzeum)

The State Jewish Museum is not confined to material from the old Jews' Town of Prague. While seeking to exterminate the Jews the Nazis set out to develop the existing Jewish Museum, then very small, into an "Exotic Museum of an extinct race", and during the period of Nazi occupation the collection grew to a total of almost 200,000 items, with synagogues in Bohemia and Moravia and elsewhere in Europe making compulsory contributions to this unique documentation of Jewish life and faith.

Opening times
Apr.–Oct., Sun.–Fri.
9 a.m.–5– p.m.;
Nov.–Mar., Sun.–Fri.
9 a.m.–4.30 p.m.

Conducted tours
On request

Josefov/
Joseph's Town
(Jews' Town)

1 Ceremonial House (Obřadní síň)
2 Klaus Synagogue (Klausova synagóga)
3 Pinkas Synagogue (Pinkasova synagóga)
4 Old-New Synagogue (Staronová synagóga)
5 High Synagogue (Vysoká synagóga)
6 Jewish Town Hall (Židovská radnice)
7 Maisl Synagogue (Maislová synagóga)
8 Spanish Synagogue (Španělská synagóga)

100 m
110 yds

Josefov

Jewish Town Hall
(Židovská radnice),
Maislova 18

The Jewish Town Hall is now the headquarters of the Jewish Community of Prague and of the Council of Jewish Communities in Czechoslovakia.

The Town Hall, presented to the Jewish community by Mordechaj Markus Maisl, Burgomaster of the Jews' Town in the time of Rudolf II, was built in 1586 by Pankraz Roder in Renaissance style, and in 1765 was remodelled in Baroque style by Josef Schlesinger. The extension at the south end was added in the first decade of the 20th c. On the north gable, under the wooden tower, is a clock with Hebrew figures; the hands go anti-clockwise, since Hebrew is read from right to left.

High Synagogue
(Vysoká synagóga),
Cervená 4

The High Synagogue, originally belonging to the Jewish Town Hall, is used by the State Jewish Museum for special exhibitions.

The High Synagogue was built by Pankraz Roder in 1586 as a square hall in Renaissance style. In the 19th c. it was separated from the Town Hall and given its own entrance from the street and staircase. The main room on the first floor was enlarged in the 17th c. and remodelled in neo-Renaissance style in the 19th. With its beautiful stellar vaulting this room – a characteristic example of Jewish religious architecture – is in sharp contrast to the plain exterior of the synagogue.

Old-New Synagogue
(Staronová synagóga)

Facing the High Synagogue is the Old-New Synagogue, the only synagogue of its period in Europe which is still in use for worship. The origin of the name is unknown.

The oldest part is the Early Gothic south hall, originally the main hall of the synagogue, to which a two-aisled hall in Cistercian Gothic style was added in the 13th c. The five-ribbed vaulting is unique in Bohemian architecture. The brick gable of the synagogue dates from the 15th c., the original timber gable having been destroyed in the great fire of 1338. The women's galleries were completed in the 17th and 18th c. (the main hall being reserved for men). The large flag was presented by the Emperor Ferdinand II in 1648 in recognition of the Jewish community's contribution to the fight against the Swedes during the Thirty Years War. In a Torah shrine on the east side of the hall is a parchment scroll of the Pentateuch, the five Books of Moses. In the centre of the hall stands the pulpit, set apart by a 15th c. screen. The Hebrew inscriptions on the walls refer to a renovation of the synagogue in 1618.

In the gardens adjoining the synagogue is a statue of Moses by František Bílek (1872–1941).

Klaus Synagogue
(Klausová synagóga)

From the Old-New Synagogue the street called U starého hřbitova (By the Old Cemetery) leads to the Klaus Synagogue. The Klaus Synagogue, a Baroque building erected in 1694 and remodelled externally in 1884, houses an exhibition concerning the work of the scholars who lived in the Jews' Town. Rabbi Löw ben Bezalel, one of the leading Jewish philosophers of the 17th c., taught in this synagogue.

Ceremonial Hall

To the right of the entrance to the Old Jewish Cemetery is the neo-Romanesque Ceremonial Hall, which is used for special exhibitions. On permanent display here are children's drawings from the Theresienstadt (Terezín) concentration camp.

The Old-New Synagogue (left) and the Jewish Town Hall (right) ▶

Gravestones in the Old Jewish Cemetery

Old Jewish Cemetery
(Starý židovsky hřbitov)

The Old Jewish Cemetery ranks with the Old-New Synagogue as one of the most important features of the old Jews' Town – and, as some would have it, one of the "ten most interesting sights in the world". It was established in the first half of the 15th c. and remained in use until 1787. Under its elder trees are no fewer than 20,000 gravestones. The restricted area of the cemetery was inadequate for the large numbers of burials, and additional earth had to be brought in to accommodate more graves. The result is that in places there are anything up to nine superimposed layers of burials. Hence the extraordinary accumulation of gravestones, huddled together in picturesque confusion.

The Hebrew inscriptions on the gravestones give the name of the dead man and of his father (in the case of women the husband's name as well), together with the dates of death and burial and a recital (sometimes in verse) of the dead person's good works. The reliefs on the gravestones frequently symbolise his name (e.g. a stag if his name is Hirsch, a bear if his name is Bär) or occupation (a doctor's instruments, a tailor's scissors), or may depict other symbols such as hands in the attitude of benediction, sacred vessels (for members of priestly families), grapes (for members of the tribe of Israel), crowns or pine-cones.

The oldest gravestone is that of the scholar and poet Avigdor Karo (d. 1439), who lived through the pogrom of 1389 and wrote an elegy on it.

A sarcophagus carved with the figures of lions marks the tomb of the learned Rabbi Jehuda Löw ben Bezalel (1609).

Other notable graves are those of Mordechaj Markus Maisl, Burgomaster of the Jews' Town (d. 1601), the historian and astronomer David Gans (d. 1613), the learned Joseph Schelomo Delmedigo (d. 1655) and the scholar and bibliophile David Oppenheim (d. 1736). One of the most beautiful and most richly decorated is that of Heudele Bassevi (d. 1628), wife of Jakob Bassevis, Treasurer of the Waldstein family.

The pebbles accumulated on many of the graves are deposited by friends and relations of the dead person in token of respect and esteem. Pious visitors throw notes into the tomb of Rabbi Löw expressing wishes which they ask the wonder-working Rabbi to fulfil.

The Pinkas Synagogue (at present in course of reconstruction: entrance only through the cemetery), on the south side of the Old Jewish Cemetery, was originally established in a house which the Horowitz family, the leading family of the Jewish community, had bought from Rabbi Pinkas in the 14th c. In 1535 Salman Munka Horowitz built a synagogue in Late Gothic style, which Juda Goldschmied de Herz remodelled in the style of the Late Renaissance in 1625, adding a women's gallery, a vestibule and a meeting-room.

Pinkas Synagogue
(Pinkasova synagóga)

Architecturally the Pinkas Synagogue is the finest of the Prague synagogues. Archaeological excavation has confirmed that the building dates from the 11th or 12th c. and that there was a ritual bath here.

After the Nazi persecutions of 1939–45, which practically wiped out the Jewish population, the "Memorial of the 77,297" was erected (1950–58), listing the names of all those who were killed.

This synagogue was founded by Mordechaj Markus Maisl, Burgomaster of the Jews' Town in the time of Rudolf II, as a

Maisl Synagogue
(Maislova synagóga)

Pinkas Synagogue: the "Memorial of the 77,297"

69

Maisl Synagogue: silver from Bohemian synagogues

family place of prayer; the architects were Joseph Wahl and Juda Goldschmied. It is a three-aisled Renaissance building (1590–92) with 20 columns supporting the roof. It was re-modelled in neo-Gothic style by Alfred Grotte between 1893 and 1905.

The Maisl Synagogue houses an exhibition of silver from 153 Bohemian synagogues and private houses. The collection includes ornaments for Torah scrolls, breastplates, crowns, Torah pointers, cult objects, including spice-boxes and etrog boxes, cups, goblets and candlesticks. This is a magnificent display of Bohemian silversmiths' work of the 17th to 19th c. and work by superb Nuremberg, Augsburg and Viennese craftsmen of the Baroque and Rococo periods.

Spanish Synagogue
(Španělská synagóga)
Dušni 12

The Spanish Synagogue contains a unique collection (due to be transferred to the High Synagogue) of ritual Jewish textiles: 2000 Torah wrappers (the earliest dating from 1592), 6000 Torah mantles, Torah ribbons, rabbis' and cantors' robes, brides' dresses, wedding girdles, caps, etc. The building occupies the site of Prague's first synagogue, known as the Old School.

The name of the synagogue comes from a group of Jews who fled from the Inquisition in Spain and settled in Prague. It was given its present Moorish-style form, with an imposing dome and stucco decoration imitated from the Alhambra, between 1882 and 1893.

Kampa Island   C5

Location
Malá Strana, Praha 1

Kampa Island is the swathe of green which extends along the left bank of the Vltava from 1st May Bridge to the Mánes

Bridge, separated from the Lesser Quarter by the idyllic (but in the past also dangerous) arm of the river known as the Čertovka or Devil's Brook. The western end of the Charles Bridge crosses the island, and some of its houses have foundations built against the piers of the original Judith Bridge. To the north of the Charles Bridge the Čertovka flows between two lines of houses which are often referred to as the "Venice of Prague" (Pražské Benátky).

In earlier times the island was marshy, with some land laid out as gardens, and the first houses were not built until the 15th c. The Čertovka then served to drive mill-wheels – still to be seen at the Charles Bridge (see entry) and the bridge leading to Grand Prior's Square (Velkopřevorské náměstí).

The attractions of Kampa Island are its pottery markets, the pleasant walks it affords and the fine views of the Vltava with the Střelecký ostrov (Marksman's Island), the Charles Bridge, the Old Town and the garden fronts of some of the palaces in the Lesser Quarter. The large park in this area was created by amalgamating the old palace gardens.

Just by the Charles Bridge is a Late Gothic figure of Roland, reconstructed by L. Šimek in 1884, which once marked the boundary between the Lesser Quarter, governed by the Magdeburg legal code, and the Old Town, governed by the Nuremberg code.

Metro
Malostranská

Trams
5, 9, 12, 22

---

*Karlovo náměstí

See Charles Square

**Karlův most

See Charles Bridge

**Karlštejn Castle (Hrad Karlštejn)

Above the little wine-producing town of Karlštejn (pop. 1200) rears Karlštejn Castle, the most celebrated of the Bohemian castles. It was built by the Emperor Charles IV between 1348 and 1357 as a place of safety in which the Crown Jewels of the Holy Roman Empire, the royal insignia of Bohemia and numerous relics could be kept. It was partially rebuilt in the 15th and 16th c. and was restored, with numerous alterations, between 1888 and 1904 (architects Friedrich Schmidt and Josef Mocker). The conducted tour starts in the Castellan's Courtyard, which has been fitted out for use as an open-air theatre.

Distance
28 km (17 miles) SW

Opening times
Open-air performances: May–Aug./Sept., Sat. and Sun. 7–11 p.m.

Castellan's Lodging
The Castellan's Lodging is on the south side of the courtyard. The lower parts of the building date from the 15th c.

Well Tower (Studniční věž)
At the westernmost tip of the castle are the old domestic offices and the large Well-Tower, with a 90 m (295 ft) deep well.

Karlštejn Castle

Karlštejn Castle

Imperial Palace (Císařský palác)
From the Castellan's Courtyard a large gateway leads into the narrow Inner Ward (Hradní nadvoří), on the right of which is the Imperial Palace. A staircase, far right, leads up to the first floor. In the first room are casts of the fine busts from the triforium of St Vitus's Cathedral (see Hradčany) and illustrative material (mostly photographs) on Charles IV and Prague as it was in his reign. In the second room are remains of stained-glass windows from the Holy Cross Chapel, pictures (including a diptych by Tommaso da Modena, second half of 14th c.), sculpture and architectural models illustrating the history of the castle.

Of the former Imperial apartments on the second floor only the study, with fine panelling, has been preserved. The half-timbered top storey with the women's quarters was replaced during the restoration work by a wooden wall-walk.

St Nicholas's Chapel
This chapel at the east end of the Imperial Palace is not open to the public.

St Mary's Tower (Mariánská věž)
This tower stands immediately north of the Imperial Palace. On the second floor (reached by a staircase in the thickness of the wall) is the Capitular Church of St Mary, which has a painted timber ceiling and wall-paintings (some dating from the 14th c.) of scenes from the Apocalypse and portraits of Charles IV.

In the south-west corner of the tower is the vaulted Chapel of St Catherine. This originally had wall-paintings, which Charles IV caused to be replaced by a facing of rare stones.

Great Tower or Keep (Velká věž)
On the highest point of the castle rock is the massive Great Tower, 37 m (121 ft) high, which is connected with St Mary's Tower by a wooden gangway (originally there was a drawbridge).

Holy Cross Chapel (Kaple svatého Kříže)
This chapel, on the second floor, was consecrated about 1360. A gilded iron screen divides it into two parts; visitors cannot enter the chancel. Its low vaulted ceiling is entirely covered with gilding and set with glass stars. On the walls, above the racks of candle-holders (for 1330 candles), are more than 2200 semi-precious stones set in gilded plaster and 128 painted wooden panels by Master Theoderich (behind which relics were originally preserved). Behind the altar is a niche in which the German Imperial Crown Jewels (now in the Treasury of the Hofburg in Vienna) and later also the Bohemian royal insignia (now in the Crown Chamber in St Vitus's Cathedral: see Hradčany) were kept.

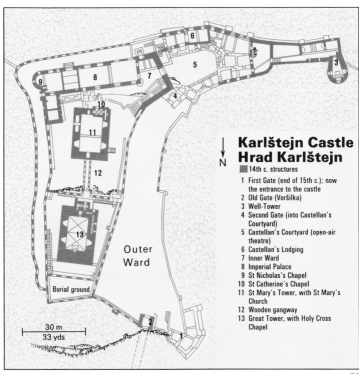

Karlštejn Castle
Hrad Karlštejn

■ 14th c. structures

1 First Gate (end of 15th c.); now the entrance to the castle
2 Old Gate (Voršilka)
3 Well-Tower
4 Second Gate (into Castellan's Courtyard)
5 Castellan's Courtyard (open-air theatre)
6 Castellan's Lodging
7 Inner Ward
8 Imperial Palace
9 St Nicholas's Chapel
10 St Catherine's Chapel
11 St Mary's Tower, with St Mary's Church
12 Wooden gangway
13 Great Tower, with Holy Cross Chapel

Outer Ward

Burial ground

30 m
33 yds

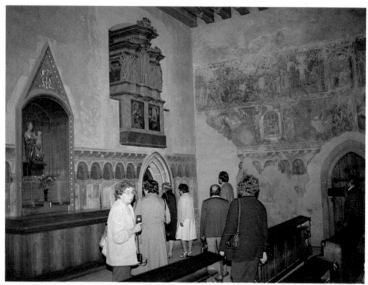

In St Mary's Tower, Karlštejn Castle

Kinsky Palace (Palác Kinských), D5(G10)
Graphic Collection of National Gallery
(Grafická sbírka Národní galerie)

Location
Staroměstské náměstí
(Old Town Square) 12,
Staré Město, Praha 1

Metro
Staroměstská

Trams
5, 9, 19, 29

The Kinsky Palace now houses the National Gallery's Collection of Graphic Art, with a fine collection on permanent display and periodic special exhibitions.

The palace is a Late Baroque building with fine Rococo features, erected on the foundations of earlier Romanesque buildings. Originally designed by Kilian Ignaz Dientzenhofer, it was completed by Anselmo Lurago (1755–65). The main front is almost neo-Classical in style, with its rich stucco decoration, projecting bays framed in pilasters and two pediments. Across the front, borne on the columns flanking the two entrances, is a balcony (from which speeches were made on special occasions). Fronting the attic storey are eight mythological figures (four erect, four reclining) by Ignaz Platzer the Elder. Rococo influence is shown by the delicately articulated window-framings with the characteristic rocaille motif. The three side wings in Empire style are later additions.

Klaus Synagogue

See Josefov

Kinsky Palace

*Knights of the Cross Square (Křižovnické náměstí)   C5(F10)

Knights of the Cross Square, one of Prague's most picturesque squares, came into being in the 16th c. at the end of the Charles Bridge (see entry). The traditional coronation procession of the Bohemian kings passed through the square. On its east side is St Salvator's Church, on its north side the Knights' Church of St Francis.

The Military Order of the Knights of the Cross with the Red Star developed out of a brotherhood of hospitallers in the period of the Crusades; it was mainly active in Silesia, Bohemia and Moravia.

Location
Staré Město, Praha 1

Metro
Staroměstská

Tram
17

St Salvator's Church, on the east side of Knights of the Cross Square, was originally a Jesuit church within the Clementinum (see entry) complex. It was built in Renaissance style betweeen 1578 and 1601. The Baroque porch was added in 1638–59 by Carlo Lurago and Francesco Caratti; the vases and statues of saints were the work of Johann Georg Bendl (1659). The towers were built in 1714 (architect F. M. Maňka). The ceiling-painting of the four quarters of the world is by K. Kovár (1748).

St Salvator's Church
(Kostel svatého Salvátora)

This Baroque church, which belonged to the Order of the Knights of the Cross, was built by Jean-Baptiste Mathey in 1679–89 on the foundations of an Early Gothic church of which some remains survive underground. The façade, in the manner of the French pre-Classical school, is decorated with

Church of St Francis Seraphicus (Kostel svatého Františka Serafinského)

statues of angels and the patron saints of Bohemia. The figures of the Virgin and St John of Nepomuk in front of the entrance are from the workshop of M. W. Jäckel (1722).

Notable features of the richly decorated and furnished interior are the large fresco of the Last Judgement (by V. V. Reiner, 1722) in the dome, the altar-piece by J. K. Liška and M. L. Willmann and a 15th c. Gothic Madonna beside the side altar. Outside the church is the Vintners' Column, by Johann Georg Bendl, with a statue of St Wenceslas (1676).

Monument to Charles IV

Between St Francis's Church and the Old Town Bridge Tower (see Charles Bridge) is a cast-iron statue of Charles IV, erected in 1848 on the 500th anniversary of Prague University.

Lesser Quarter (Malá Strana)   B4–6

Location
Malá Strana, Praha 1

Metro
Malostranská

Trams
12, 22

The Lesser Quarter or Little Town is the name given to the district of Prague which was originally the "lesser town of Prague" founded in 1257, during the reign of Přemysl Ottokar II. In the reign of Charles IV the settlement grew; the churches of the Přemyslid period, some of them going back to the Romanesque period, were rebuilt, and the little town was enclosed within walls which extended as far as the Hunger Wall on Petřín Hill (see entry).

In the 15th and 16th c. the Lesser Quarter was devastated by three major fires, which led to further building and rebuilding. After the catastrophic fire of 1541 the town took on the aspect of a princely capital: wealthy nobles came here to live, and magnificent churches were built. After the Battle of the White Mountain in 1620, in which the forces of the Catholic League defeated the Protestants, many noble families from other parts of the Empire moved into Bohemia, and this gave a further impulse to the development of the Lesser Quarter. Whole streets and large areas of gardens were destroyed to make way for the splendid mansions of the Habsburg and Catholic nobility, such as the Nostitz Palace, the Waldstein Palace and the Buquoy Palace (see entries). Each noble family sought to establish a palace near the Hradčany (see entry) and if possible to surpass it in splendour.

St Nicholas's Church (see Lesser Quarter Square) with its dome became the dominant feature of the town, which otherwise spread out in horizontal lines. This was the decisive period in the building history of the Lesser Quarter, giving it its distinctly Baroque character.

The attraction of the quarter was enhanced by numbers of small squares including Waldstein Square, Grand Prior's Square (Velkopřevorské náměstí) and Maltese or Five Churches Square and by the gardens of monasteries and palaces, most of which are now open to the public.

From Bridge Lane (Mostecká) the coronation processions of the Bohemian kings crossed Lesser Quarter Square (see entry) and along what is now Neruda Street (Nerudova) to the Hradčany (see entry).

Lesser Quarter Bridge Towers

See Charles Bridge

*Lesser Quarter Square (Malostranské náměstí)　　B4

Location
Malá Strana, Praha 1

Metro
Malostranská

Trams
12, 22

Lesser Quarter Square, the focal point of the Lesser Quarter since its earliest days, is divided into two smaller squares by the buildings around St Nicholas's Church.

In the lower square are such notable buildings as the Lesser Quarter Town Hall and the Late Baroque Kaiserstein Palace (U Petzoldu; *c.* 1700) on the east side and the Rococo house "At the Sign of the Stone Table" in the middle.

The main feature of the upper square is the Liechtenstein Palace (1791), now a Communist Party school.

Lesser Quarter Town Hall (Malostranská radnice)

The Town Hall of the Lesser Quarter has stood on this site since the late 15th c. The important negotiations on the Bohemian Confession were held here in 1575.

In its present form the Town Hall dates from the Late Renaissance (1617–22). The doorway with the town's coat of arms was added in 1660.

St Nicholas's Church (Chram svatého Mikuláše)

Formerly a Jesuit church, St Nicholas's Church occupies the site of an earlier Gothic church with the same dedication. Its construction was the work of three generations of the best Baroque architects of Prague. The mighty nave with its side

The Lesser Quarter Town Hall

St Nicholas's Church Chrám svatého Mikuláše

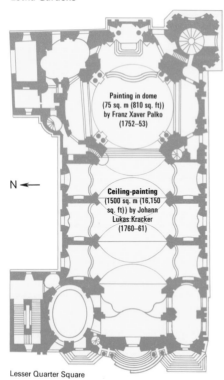

Painting in dome
(75 sq. m (810 sq. ft))
by Franz Xaver Palko
(1752–53)

N ←

Ceiling-painting
(1500 sq. m (16,150
sq. ft)) by Johann
Lukas Kracker
(1760–61)

Lesser Quarter Square

St Nicholas was a 4th-c. Bishop of Myra in Asia Minor who was regarded in medieval times as the patron saint of municipal administration and the guardian of justice.

The centre of the ceiling-paiting is dominated by the figure of the Saint, surrounded by angels, with his crosier in his left hand and his right hand raised in blessing. One scene shows a priest distributing phials of the wonder-working oil dispensed by the Saint. Another scene depicts Nicholas giving money to a poor man who is reduced to selling his daughter for gold.

A scene on the right-hand side refers to an occasion during the wars of the 14th c. when St Nicholas saved three Romans from execution by his intervention. On the left-hand side is a coastal landscape, alluding to the Saint's role as protector of seafarers and merchants. Coastal and harbour scenes were much favoured by the burghers of Prague during this period.

chapels, galleries and vaulting was built by Christoph Dientzenhofer (1704–11), the choir with its dome by Kilian Ignaz Dientzenhofer (1737–52), and the tall tower which completed the church by Anselmo Lurago (1756).

The sumptuously decorated interior achieves its awesome effect mainly through its superb frescoes. The ceiling-painting in the nave (by Johann Lukas Kracker, 1760–61) depicts scenes from the life of St Nicholas. The dome has representations of the Glorification of St Nicholas and the Last Judgement by Franz Xaver Palko (1752–53), who was also responsible, together with Joseph Hager, for the wall-paintings in the choir. The sculpture in the nave and choir and the figure of St Nicholas on the high altar are by Ignaz Platzer the Elder, the pulpit by Richard and Peter Prachner (1765).

Letná Gardens (Letenské sady)   C/D3/4

Location
Na baště svatého Tomáše,
Hradčany, Praha 6
Konstelní,
Holešovice, Praha 7

North-east of the Hradčany (see entry), above the left bank of the Vltava, rises Letná Hill (Summer Hill) with its beautiful gardens. From Svatopluk Čech Bridge a stepped path (256 steps in all) leads up to the outlook platform on the massive base which once supported a 30 m (100 ft) high monument to

Stalin (pulled down in 1962), and now affords panoramic views of Prague, Petřín Hill (see entry) and St Vitus's Cathedral (see Hradčany).

Near the east end of the gardens (formerly Belvedere Park) is the Praha Restaurant, which was originally part of the Czechoslovak section of the 1958 Brussels International Exhibition and was re-erected on its present site after the exhibition. From here, too, there is a good view of Prague, although the Hradčany is obscured.

On the north side of the gardens, in the Holešovice district, near the exit from the road tunnel under Letná Hill, stands the National Museum of Technology (see entry).

Trams
8, 12, 17, 18, 20, 22, 23, 25, 26, 31

Lobkowitz Palace (Lobkovický palác)   B4/5

The Lobkowitz Palace, built by Giovanni Battista Alliprandi in Early Baroque style, was altered and had an additional storey added to the side wings by I. Palliardi in 1703–07. The main front is finely articulated, with a massive doorway, a pediment decorated with sculpture and an attic storey with statues. The interior has rich painted decoration.

Still more interesting is the rear façade, with a cylindrical projection and a *sala terrena* leading into the grand courtyard. On the roof above the projecting bay is an unusual architectural feature – an ornamental pond. From the grand courtyard enclosed by the three wings of the palace a gateway enriched by sculpture gives access to the English-style park (fine views). The palace is now occupied by the Embassy of the Federal Republic of Germany.

Location
Vlašská 19,
Malá Strana, Praha 1

Trams
12, 22

*Loreto (Loreta)   A4

From Hradčany Square (see entry) a street lined with old burghers' houses, Loreto Street (Loretánská ulička) – in which Peter Parler, the architect of St Vitus's Cathedral, once lived – leads to Loreto Square, which ranks with Knights of the Cross Square (see entry) and one or two other squares as one of the most beautiful spots in Prague.

Along the south-west side of the square extends the 150 m (490 ft) long façade, articulated by 30 tall pilasters, of the Černín Palace (1669–97). The palace, with a sumptuously decorated interior (ceiling-frescoes by V. V. Reiner), the palace gardens on the north side and the Orangery are now occupied by departments of the Foreign Ministry.

On the east side of the square, which falls steeply towards the north, is the old shrine and pilgrimage centre of Loreto.

Location
Loretánské náměstí
(Loreto Square),
Hradčany, Praha 1

Trams
22, 23

Loreto Shrine

Prague's Loreto Shrine is the best known in Bohemia. During the Counter-Reformation some 50 Loreto shrines were built in Bohemia, on the model of the Santa Casa shrine at Loreto in Italy, in order to increase the appeal of Catholicism to ordinary people.

The main front (1721 onwards) was designed by Christoph and Kilian Ignaz Dientzenhofer. The statue of St Felix, by

Loreto: the best-known Loreto shrine in Bohemia

Johann Friedrich Kohl also dates from 1721. The bell-tower, in Early Baroque style, is earlier; it contains a carillon (installed by P. Neumann in 1694) which plays Marian hymns every hour in summer. The 27 bells were cast in Amsterdam in 1694.

Loreto Chapel

In the two-storey cloister with its central fountain is the Loreto Chapel (Loretánská kaple), the architectural and spiritual heart of the whole complex. The chapel was founded by Countess Benigna Katharina von Lobkowitz in 1626. The sculpture and stucco reliefs depicting scenes from the lives of the Old Testament Prophets were the work of J. Agosta, J. B. Colombo and G. B. Cometa (1664). The Casa Santa contains pictures of scenes from the life of the Virgin, a silver altar and a carved cedarwood Madonna. The lower cloister has frescoes by F. A. Scheffler (1750). In it are altars with figures of saints and seven chapels.

Church of the Nativity

On the east side of the cloister is the Church of the Nativity (Kostel Narození Páně), begun by Christoph Dientzenhofer in 1717, contined by his son Kilian Ignaz and completed by Georg Aichbauer in 1735. The interior is sumptuously decorated, with ceiling-paintings by V. V. Reiner ("Presentation in the Temple", 1735–36) and J. A. Schöpf ("Adoration of the Shepherds", "Adoration of the Kings", 1742).

Treasury

The Treasury, on the upper floor of the cloister, contains vestments and valuable 17th and 18th c. monstrances, including the famous Diamond Monstrance, made in Vienna in 1699.

From the Loreto Shrine a street runs north to the "New World" (Nový svět), a picturesque old corner of the town on Hradčany Hill. The House of the Golden Horn was occupied by the great astronomer Johannes Kepler in 1600. The Baroque House of the Golden Pear is now an attractive restaurant.

Capuchin Friary (Kapucínský klášter)

On the north side of Loreto Square, down the hill from the Černín Palace, is the first Capuchin Friary to be built in Bohemia (1600–02), in the plain architectural style of Capuchin houses. An enclosed corridor at first-floor level links it with the Loreto Shrine opposite.
Adjoining the friary is a simple church dedicated to the Virgin, which originally had 14 Gothic panel-paintings of unknown origin (now in the National Gallery). At Christmas the church attracts large numbers of worshippers with its beautiful Baroque crib (Nativity scene).

Maisl Synagogue

See Josefov

Malá Strana

See Lesser Quarter

Mánes Exhibition Hall C6

The Mánes Exhibition Hall, in Constructivist style, was built by O. Novotný in 1930 for the group of artists associated with Josef Mánes (see Notable Personalities). It is now the home of

Location
Gottwaldovo nábřeží 20,
Nové Město, Praha 1

Sculpture in the Mánes Exhibition Hall

Buses
120, 128, 134, 137, 176, 197

Trams 3, 17, 21

the Artists' Union. Attached to the exhibition hall are a restaurant and a café with a garden terrace.

Adjoining the Mánes Exhibition Hall is the Šitek Water-Tower (see entry).

Martinitz Palace

See Hradčany Square

Morzin Palace (Morzinský palác)   B4

Location
Nerudova ulice 5,
Malá strana, Praha 1

Metro
Malostranská

Trams 12, 22

In the Morzin Palace (1714), one of the finest Baroque palaces in the Lesser Quarter (see entry), the Baroque architecture of Giovanni Santini combines with the sculpture of Ferdinand Maximilian Brokoff to form a harmonious whole. The balcony is supported on figures of Moors – heraldic emblems of the Morzin family. Above the doorway are allegories of Day and Night.

Mozart Museum

See Bertramka

Municipal Museum (Muzeum hlavního města Prahy)   E5

Location
Sady Jana Švermy,
Nové Město, Praha 1

Metro
Sokolovská

Buses
135, 200, 207, 210, 233

Trams
5, 10, 14, 15, 18, 19, 24

Opening times
Tues.–Sun. 9 a.m.–5 p.m.

The Municipal Museum was built in 1898 by Antonín Balšánek and A. Wiehl in neo-Renaissance style. The decoration on the façade is by a number of different sculptors.

In the hall by the staircase hangs the face painted by Josef Mánes for the astronomical clock of the Old Town Hall (see entry), with the signs of the zodiac on the inner ring and the twelve months, symbolised by scenes of country life, on the outer ring.

The museum, originally founded in 1884, illustrates the economic, architectural and cultural history of Prague down the centuries, with furnished rooms, historic costumes, jewellery, pottery and sculpture from the Prague area and a collection of Prague house signs (see entry). An item of particular interest is a model of the town, measuring 20 sq. m (215 sq. ft), by the lithographer A. Langweil (1830), which depicts in minute detail the houses, churches and palaces of early 19th c. Prague.

*Museum of Applied Art (Umělecko-průmyslové muzeum)   C4(G9)

Location
Ulice 17. listopadu 2,
Staré Město, Praha 1

Metro
Staroměstská

The Museum of Applied Art was founded in 1884. The present neo-Renaissance building, on the west side of the Old Jewish Cemetery (see Josefov), was erected in 1897–1901 (architect Josef Schulz).

The museum has a world-famed collection of glass, porcelain and pottery, furniture of the 16th–19th c. and goldsmith's work of the 15th–19th c.

Other fields represented are textiles, measuring instruments, bookbinding, commercial art, small bronzes and coins (illustrating their historical development, with examples dating back to 700). From time to time there are well-prepared special exhibitions.

The museum has a specialised library (open to the public) on art history and applied art, including a collection of 15th c. parchments.

Buses
133, 144, 156, 197

Tram 17

Opening times
Tues.–Sun. 10 a.m.–6 p.m.

Museum of Military History

See Hradčany Square, Schwarzenberg Palace

Na Příkopě (On the Moat)   D5(G/H10)

The street named Na Příkopě, known to German-speakers as the Graben, is the busiest street in Prague, running between the lower end of Wenceslas Square (see entry) and Revolution Square (Náměstí revoluce). Na Příkopě, Wenceslas Square, Nǎrodní třída and the side streets opening off them are the commercial centre of Prague, known as the "Golden Cross", with banks, office blocks, shops, cafés, etc. The street follows the line of a stream which later became a moat between the Old and New Towns and was filled in 1760.

Coming from Wenceslas Square, the Old Town lies on the left, the New Town on the right. On the left-hand side are the State

Location
Praha 1

Metro
Můstek

Trams
5, 9, 19, 29

Sylva-Taroucca Palace

Bank of Czechoslovakia, the Children's Store, the Moskva Restaurant and the Ministry of Transport.

A little way beyond the Textile Store, the oldest department store on the New Town Side, is the Sylva-Taroucca Palace.

Sylva-Taroucca Palace

This gem of Bohemian Late Baroque architecture is now occupied by function rooms and a restaurant (tables in the garden in summer).

The palace, built by Anselmo Lurago in 1743–51 to the design of Kilian Ignaz Dientzenhofer, shows the influence of French Classical architecture, with two courtyards, a carriage entrance flanked by columns, a garden and a riding-school. The decoration of the richly articulated façade and the Rococo staircase was the work of Ignaz Platzer the Elder; the stucco-work in the interior is by Carlo Bassis.

Čedok

At No. 18 is the office of the Čedok travel agency. It occupies the old Land Bank (Zemská banka), built in 1912.

Holy Cross Church
(Kostel svatého Kříže)

Holy Cross Church, the only Empire church in Prague, was built by J. Fischer in 1816–24 for the Piarist Teaching Order. The old Piarist school is in Panská ulice.

Prague Information Service

No. 20 houses the office of the Prague Information Service (Pražska informační služba). Beyond it is the Baroque Příchovských Palace (c. 1700), which from 1875 to 1945 was "German House", the meeting-place of Prague's German population, and since then has been renamed Slav House (Slovanský dům).

National Memorial on St Vitus's Hill   F5
(Národní památnik na hoře Vitkově)

Location
Na vrchu Žižkově, Žižkov,
Praha 3

Buses
133, 135, 168

Opening times
Apr.–Oct., 9 a.m.–5 p.m.;
Nov.–Mar. 10 a.m.–4 p.m.;
Museum: Tues.–Sun.
9.30 a.m.–4.30 p.m.

The National Memorial on St Vitus's Hill, in the eastern district of Žižkov, is best reached by way of Třída Vitězného února, Husitská třída and the street called U Památniku (At the Monument), and thereafter by steps.

The National Memorial was built in 1927–32, but the interior was completed only in 1948 and subsequent years. Above a terrace which affords extensive views of Prague and the hills to the west rears a monumental equestrian statue by Bohumil Kafka (1950) of the Hussite General Jan Žižka, who defeated the Imperial forces here. Beyond it is a massive mausoleum for the Presidents of the Republic and other politicians of the post-war Communist period. The upper part is a Mourning Hall (with a large organ), and below this is the mausoleum proper, with marble sarcophagi (containing only urns) and a columbarium. Here, too, is a hall commemorating those who fell in the First World War. Under the equestrian statue lies the Tomb of the Unknown Soldier of the Second World War (one who fought at the Dukla Pass: (see Town Hall of Old Town).

At the foot of St Vitus's Hill, at the near end of U Památniku (on the right), is the Military Museum of the Czechoslovak Army (Vojenské muzeum Československé armády).

National Museum
Národní muzeum

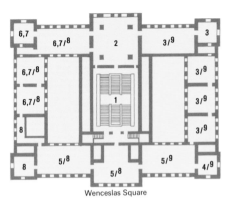

Wenceslas Square

FIRST FLOOR (PRVNÍ POSCHODÍ)

1 Statue of King George of Poděbrad (1420–71), by Ludwig Schwanthaler
2 Busts of men who have made valuable contributions to science or to the museum
3 Prehistory and archaeology
4 Numismatic department
5 Special exhibitions
6, 7 Mineralogy and petrography

SECOND FLOOR (DRUHÝ POSCHODÍ)

8 Zoology
9 Palaeontology

■ Statues

■ Busts on bases

● Busts on the walls

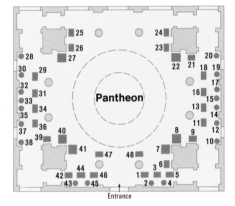

Entrance

1 Beneš z Loun (1454–1534), architect
2 Ferdinand Maximilian Brokoff (1688–1731), sculptor
3 Miroslav Tyrš (1832–84), art historian
4 Karel Škréta (1610–74), painter
5 Josef Mánes (1820–71), painter
6 Jaroslav Heyrovský (1890–1966), founder of Polar exploration
7 František Palacký (1798–1876), historian and politician
8 Tomáš Garrigue Masaryk (1850–1937), President of Czechoslovak Republic
9 Karel Havlíček Borovský (1821–56), journalist
10 Ctibor Tovačovský z Cimburka (1438–94), politician
11 František Josef Gerstner (1758–1832), physicist and technician
12 Bohuslav Balbín (1621–88)
13 Jan E. Purkyně (1787–1869)
14 Josef Ressel (1793–1857), inventor of the screw-propeller
15 Josef Dobrovský (1753–1829)
16 Pavel Josef Šafařík (1795–1861)
17 František Martin Pelci (1734–1801), historian
18 Josef Jungmann (1773–1847)
19 Karel ze Žerotína (1564–1636)
20 Viktorin Kornel ze Všehrd (1460–1520), jurist
21 František Škroup (1801–62), composer of the National Anthem
22 Jan Hus (1371–1415), Reformer
23 Antonín Dvořák (1841–1904), composer
24 Bedřich Smetana (1824–84), composer

25 Stanislav Kostka Neumann (1875–1947), poet
26 Julius Fučík (1903–43)
27 Jan Amos Komenský (1592–1670), pedagogue and Reformer
28 Daniel Adam z Veleslavína (1546–99), historian
29 Pavol Hviezdoslav (1849–1921), poet
30 Karel Jaromír Erben (1811–70), poet and historian
31 Jaroslav Vrchlický (1853–1912), poet
32 Antonín Jaroslav Puchmajer (1769–1820), poet
33 Jan Kollár (1793–1852), poet
34 Svatopluk Čech (1846–1908), poet and writer
35 Václav Matěj Kramerius (1753–1808), writer
36 Alois Jirásek (1851–1930), writer

37 František Ladislav Čelakovský (1799–1852), poet
38 Tomáš ze Štítného (1333–1405), religious philosopher
39 Petr Bezruč (1867–1958), poet
40 Jan Neruda (1834–91), poet
41 Kašpar Šternberk (1761–1838), co-founder of National Museum
42 Václav Hollar (1607–77), engraver
43 Václac Vavřinec Reiner (1689–1743), painter
44 Josef Václav Myslbek (1848–1922), sculptor
45 Petr Jan Brandl (1668–1735), painter
46 Mikoláš Aleš (1852–1913), painter
47 Eliška Krásnohorská (1847–1926), poetess
48 Božena Němcová (1820–62), writer

The National Museum, Czechoslovakia's oldest museum

National Museum (Národní muzeum)　　D6

Location
Václavské náměstí
(Wenceslas Square), Nové
Město, Praha 1

Metro
Muzeum

Tram
11

Opening times
Sat., Sun., Wed. and Thurs.
9 a.m.–5 p.m., Mon. and Fri.
9 a.m.–4 p.m.

The National Museum, founded in 1818, is Czechoslovakia's oldest museum. It incorporates the Ethnographic Museum (see entry), the Music Museum, the Náprstek Museum and the Museum of Physical Culture and Sport, all housed in separate buildings.

The main building, with its recently regilded dome, stands at the upper end of Wenceslas Square (see entry). In neo-Renaissance style, it was built between 1885 and 1890 by Josef Schulz, and houses the Natural History and Historical Museums and the Library of the National Museum (over 1·3 million volumes).

In the Pantheon, a domed hall two storeys high, are statues and busts of distinguished Czechs. The mineralogical, botanical and zoological collections are in the side wings. Of particular interest in the department of history and archaeology is a large collection of coins and medals as well as exhibits illustrating the history of the Czech theatre and puppet theatre.

National Museum of Technology (Národní technické muzeum)　　D3

Location
Kostelní ulice, Holešovice,
Praha 7

The National Museum of Technology, on the northern slopes of Letná Hill (see entry), offers a wide-ranging survey of the development of cinematography in more than 50 countries, radio and television, transport and mining. A particularly

National Museum of Technology: the transport department

impressive feature is a 600 m (650 yd) long mine shaft. In the main hall are aircraft and locomotives, as well as two cars belonging to the Emperor Francis Joseph in which the heir to the throne, Francis Ferdinand, drove to Sarajevo, where he was assassinated in 1914. In the courtyard to the right of the museum there are also a number of aircraft.

Bus
125

Opening times
Tues.–Sun. 10 a.m.–5 p.m.

National Theatre (Národní divadlo)

C6(F11)

The neo-Renaissance National Theatre, built by Josef Zítek in 1868–81 was burnt down shortly after the first performance in the theatre, but was rebuilt by Josef Schulz within two years, the cost being met by contributions from the public. The theatre "incarnates all the yearnings and aspirations of a people which after long slumber was returning, full of energy and enthusiasm, into the European intellectual community" (V. Volavka). All the leading artists of the day contributed to the interior decoration of the theatre. The figures on the attic loggias and the goddesses of victory on the main front are by B. Schnirch. The theatre was reopened after extensive restoration work in 1983.

Location
Národní třída (corner of Smetana Embankment), Nové Město, Praha 1

Trams
5, 9, 17, 22

New Town Hall

See Charles Square

The National Theatre, in neo-Renaissance style

Nostitz Palace (Nostický palác)   B5

Location
Maltézské náměstí 471, Malá
Strana, Praha 1

Trams
12, 22

The Nostitz Palace, a quadrangular structure built round a courtyard, occupies the south side of Maltese Square in the Lesser Quarter (see entry). It now houses the Netherlands Embassy and various departments of the Ministry of Culture.
This Baroque palace was built for Johann Hertwig von Nostitz, probably by Francesco Caratti, in 1658–60. The dormer windows and the statues of emperors (from the workshop of F. M. Brokoff) were added in 1720, the columned doorway (by Anton Hafenecker) after 1765. Notable features of the interior are the beautiful courtyard and the ceiling-frescoes in the principal apartments (by W. B. Ambrozzi, *c.* 1757).
The palace also houses the Dobrovský Library (formerly the Nostitz Library).

Old Jewish Cemetery

See Josefov

Old-New Synagogue

See Josefov

Old Town Bridge Tower

See Charles Bridge

Old Town Square (Staroměstske náměstí)   D5(G10)

Old Town Square ranks with the Hradčany (see entry) as one of the two most historic places in Prague. This spacious square (9000 sq. m (11,000 sq. yd)) was the market-place of the Old Town in the 11th and 12th c., and lay on the route of the traditional coronation procession of the Bohemian kings from the Vyšehrad (see entry) to the Hradčany.

The square has been the scene of great events, both glorious and tragic.

1422: The radical Hussite preacher Jan Želivský, who with his supporters from the poor quarters of the city had stormed the New Town Hall in 1419 and, with the First Defenestration of Prague, had given the signal for the Hussite Wars, is executed (memorial tablet and bust on east side of Town Hall).

1437: The Hussite officer Jan Roháč of Dubá and 56 other Hussites are executed.

1458: George of Poděbrad is elected as King of Bohemia in the Town Hall (picture by V. Brožík in Town Hall). His reign was the heyday of Bohemian independence.

1621: The 27 leaders of the Protestant rising of the nobility are executed on the orders of Ferdinand II (commemorative tablet on east side of Town Hall).

1915: 500th anniversary of the death of Jan Hus. The Jan Hus Monument (by Ladislav Šaloun), with the inscription "The truth will prevail", is unveiled.

1918: End of the monarchy. The people of Prague demonstrate in the square, calling for a Socialist Czechoslovakia.

1945: End of the Second World War; the Soviet army is given an enthusiastic reception by large crowds.

1948: Speech by Klement Gottwald on the balcony of the Kinsky Palace (see entry) proclaiming the Communist accession to power.

1968: End of the "Prague Spring". The tanks of the Warsaw Pact forces are received with Molotov cocktails and the Jan Hus Monument is draped in black.

In the basements of the buildings in Old Town Square (see Town Hall of Old Town, St Nicholas's Church, Kinskey Palace, Týn Church, St James's Church) are many remains of Romanesque houses. After the devastation caused by the flooding of the Vltava in the 11th and 12th c. the level of the Old Town was raised by the deposit of additional soil and the new houses were built on top of the old ones.

Location
Staré Město, Praha 1

Metro
Staroměstská

Trams
5, 9, 19, 29

Palace of Culture (Paláce kultury)   D8

The ultra-modern Palace of Culture (1981), a little way east of the Vyšehrad (see entry), is a fine example of contemporary Czech architecture. With its area of almost 280,000 sq. m (3,000,000 sq. ft) on several floors, it can accommodate a great variety of events – mass rallies, concerts, theatrical performances, exhibitions, entertainments, dances.

Location
Vyšehrad, Praha 2

Metro
Gottwaldova

The central element in the building is the Congress Hall, which can be converted into an auditorium for an audience of up to 3000. The mighty organ is a reminder that the hall can also be used for concerts (e.g. during the Prague Spring Festival).

Congress Hall

For smaller events there are four smaller halls, equipped with every technical refinement. There is also a hall specially designed for exhibitions as well as a number of conference rooms of different sizes.

Other facilities

Within the Palace of Culture are the select Panorama Restaurant and the elegant Vyšehrad Café, both affording fine views. An exclusive rendezvous for night-life enthusiasts is the Krystal night club.

Restaurant, etc.

*Petřín Hill   A/B5

From the gardens of Strahov Abbey (see entry) a path climbs up through the old seminary gardens to the top of Petřín Hill, from which there is a magnificent view of Prague.
On the hill – an eastern outlier of the White Mountain (see entry) – are the Petřín Tower, St Lawrence's Church, the People's Observatory, the Mirror Maze and the Hunger Wall.

Location
Malá Strana, Praha 1

Trams
5, 9, 12, 22, 23

This 60 m (200 ft) high tower was erected for the Prague Industrial Exhibition of 1891 on a model of the Eiffel Tower, and now serves as a television tower. From the upper gallery (384 m (1260 ft) above sea-level) there are far-ranging sea views of Prague and Central Bohemia.

Petřín Tower
(Petřínská rozhledna)

Originally Romanesque (1135), St Lawrence's Church was rebuilt between 1735 and 1770 (architect I. Palliardi) in Baroque style as a domed church with two towers. Hence the German name of Petřín Hill, Laurenziberg or St Lawrence's Hill.

St Lawrence's Church
(Kostel svatého Vavřince)

Near the church is a pavilion containing a panorama of the Prague students' fight against the Swedes in 1648 (by Karl and Adolf Liebscher, 1898).

Pavilion

A small building which formed part of the old Charles Gate now houses the Mirror Maze (open Apr.–Oct., daily 9 a.m.–7 p.m.), which was constructed at the same time as the Petřín Tower.

Mirror Maze
(Bludiště)

From the top of the hill the old town wall, built in 1360 in the reign of Charles IV, runs down to the foot. It is called the Hunger Wall from a legend that it was built to provide employment in the fight against hunger.

Hunger Wall

The People's Observatory contains an astronomical exhibition, and is open in the evening to allow amateur astronomers to pursue their hobby.

People's Observatory
(Hvězdárna)

Pinkas Synagogue

See Josefov

◄ *Old Town Square, with the Town Hall (left) and the Town Church*

The Hunger Wall on Petřín Hill

Portheimka B6

Location
Třída S. M. Kirova 12,
Smíchov, Praha 5

Trams
5, 12

This Baroque mansion was built by Kilian Ignaz Dientzenhofer in 1729 for his own family and later passed into the hands of a Prague industrialist named Portheim. The ceiling-frescoes in the central room are by V. V. Reiner. Part of the house was pulled down in 1884 to make room for St Wenceslas's Church. The house is now occupied by Gallery D, where occasional exhibitions are mounted.

*Powder Tower (Prašná brána) D5(H10)

Location
Náměstí Republiky
(Republic Square), Staré
Město, Praha 1

Metro
Můstek

Trams
3, 5, 9, 10, 19, 26, 29

Opening times
Sat., Sun. and pub. hol.,
May–Sep. 10 a.m.–6 p.m.
Apr. and Oct. 10 a.m.–5 p.m.

This 65 m (215 ft) high Late Gothic tower, through which the trade route from the south entered Prague, was modelled on the Old Town Bridge Tower (See Charles Bridge) and formed part of the fortifications of the Old Town. The tower, successor to an earlier 13th c. fortified gateway, was built (1475 onwards) by M. Rejsek for King Vladislav Jagiello at the behest of the Municipal Council. After Vladislav moved his residence to the Hradčany (see entry) the importance of the Powder Tower declined.

The tower acquired its present name in the 18th c., when it was used as a powder-magazine. The sculptural decoration was badly damaged during Frederick the Great's siege of Prague in

Powder Tower ▶

1757. In 1875 the tower was reconstructed in neo-Gothic style by J. Mocker and given a new steeple roof and wall-walk. The sculpture – which includes portraits of Bohemian kings – was the work of J. Šimek, A. Wildt and other sculptors.

Closed
Nov.–Mar.

St Agnes's Convent (Klášter Anežsky)   D4

St Agnes's Convent, which now houses collections belonging to the National Gallery and the Museum of Applied Art, is Prague's first Early Gothic building.

The convent was founded in 1234 by Agnes, a sister of King Wenceslas I, for the Order of Poor Clares (Franciscan nuns). Agnes later entered the Order and became the convent's first Abbess. Subsequently the churches of St Barbara (1250–80) and St Francis (c. 1250) and the conventual buildings were erected. The tower of the convent dates from the 14th c.

After the dissolution of religious houses in the reign of the Emperor Joseph II (1782) the convent fell into a state of disrepair. It has been restored in recent years after extensive preliminary archaeological investigation. On the ground floor is an exhibition of Bohemian applied art, with a fascinating range of beautiful objects, from Rococo and Empire to neo-Renaissance and Jugendstil (Art Nouveau).

Room 16 is devoted to 19th c. Czech painting. Of particular interest are the portraits by Antonín Machek (1775–1844), the landscapes of August Piepenhagen (1791–1868), the still-life paintings of Josef Navrátil (1798–1865) and an extensive display of the works of Josef Mánes (see Notable Personalities), the leading painter of the period.

Also worth looking at are the works of the "National Theatre generation" (Rooms 17–20), including landscapes by Antonín Chittussi (1847–91) and Historical pictures by Václav Brožik (1851–1901).

Rooms 21 and 22 contain works by artists of the end of the 19th c. – genre pictures by Hanuš Schwaiger (1854–1912) and the still-life paintings, bathed in a poetic twilight, of Jakub Schikaneder (1855–1924).

Location
Anežská ulice, Staré Město, Praha 1

Buses
125, 133, 144, 156, 187

Trams
3, 26, 29

Opening times
Tues.–Sun. 10 a.m.–6 p.m.

St Barbara's Church

See St Agnes's Convent

St Cajetan's Church

See Thun-Hohenstein Palace

St Catherine's Church (Kostel svaté Kateřiny)   D7

This church, which formerly belonged to St Catherine's Convent is now used as an exhibition hall for the sculpture collection of the Municipal Lapidarium. When remodelling the church in 1737–41 F. M. Kaňka incorporated the original

Location
Kateřinská ulice (entrance in Viničná ulice), Nové Město, Praha 1

◀ *St Agnes's Convent, Prague's oldest Gothic building*

St Agnes's Convent

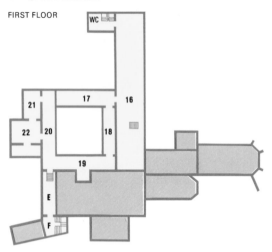

FIRST FLOOR

St Agnes's Convent
Bývalý klášter Anežsky

National Gallery
19th c. Czech Painting
Museum of Applied Art
19th c. Bohemian Applied Art

GROUND FLOOR

Gothic octagonal tower in the new Baroque structure. The slender form of the tower has led it to be called "Prague's minaret". The interior has frescoes by V. V. Reiner ("Life of St Catherine") and stucco-work by B. Spinetti.
The conventual buildings are now occupied by the regional psychiatric clinic.

Metro
I. P. Pavlova

Opening times
In summer, Sat. 1 a.m.–
6 p.m. Sun. 10 a.m.–6 p.m.

---

*St Clement's Church (Kostel svatého Klimenta) C5(F/G10)

The Baroque Church of St Clement, built between 1711 and 1715, is part of the Clementinum (see entry) complex and is linked with the Latin Chapel by an iron grille. The sculpture in the interior is among the finest Baroque sculpture in Bohemia. The eight figures of Evangelists and Fathers of the Church are by Matthias Bernhard Braun, as is the wood-carving on the side altars, the pulpit and the confessional. The altar-piece by Peter Brandl represents St Lienhard.
St Clement's is now used by the Greek Catholic community as a guest-house.

Location
Karlova ulice, Staré Město,
Praha 1

Metro
Staroměstská

Bus
197

Tram
17

SS. Cyril and Methodius, Church C6
(Kostel svatého Cyrila a Metoděje)

This Baroque church, built by Kilian Ignaz Dientzenhofer in about 1740, was originally dedicated to St Charles Borromeo. In 1935 it changed its dedication on being taken over by the Czechoslovak Hussite Church. The interior has stucco decoration by M. I. Palliardi.
The crypt of the church was used as a hiding-place by the Czech paratroops who killed Reinhard Heydrich, the German "Protector" of Bohemia and Moravia, at Lidice in 1942. The Nazi authorities reacted with predictable brutality: Lidice was razed to the ground, all the male inhabitants over 16 were shot and the women were sent to concentration camps and the children to indoctrination camps. None of the Resistance fighters in the crypt survived. They are commemorated by a tablet bearing their names.
Diagonally across the street is the Church of St Wenceslas in Zderaz (see entry) and Charles Square (see entry) with its various features of interest (Faust House, St Ignatius's Church, New Town Hall) is only a few paces away.

Location
Resslova ulice, Nové Město,
Praha 1

Buses
120, 128, 134, 137, 176

Trams
3, 4, 14, 15, 16, 17, 18, 21,
27

St Francis's Church

See Knights of the Cross Square
See St Agnes's Convent

St Gallus's Church (Kostel svatého Havla) D5(G10)

St Gallus's Church was founded in 1232, at the same time as the settlement of South Germans known as "St Gallus's Town", and was completed in 1263 to become one of the four

Location
Havelská ulice, Staré Město,
Praha 1

97

St George's Basilica

Metro
Můstek

Trams
5, 9, 19, 29

parish churches of the Old Town. It was rebuilt in High Gothic style in 1353, and further remodelling in the 18th c. gave it its curving façade and twin towers.

The Baroque interior has fine altar-pieces and (on the left) a carved Pietà, probably by F. M. Brokoff. In the side chapel to the right is the tomb of the painter Karel Škréta.

From 1363 the Austrian preacher Konrad von Waldhausen, a forerunner of the Reformer Jan Hus, officiated in this church at the wish of Charles IV.

St George's Basilica

See Hradčany

St Giles's Church (Kostel svatého Jiljí)   D5(G10)

Location
Husova třída, Staré Město,
Praha 1

Metro
Staroměstská

Trams
5, 9, 29

Originally Romanesque, St Giles's Church was rebuilt in Gothic style between 1339 and 1371. It belonged to the Hussite Utraquists (who believed that laymen should receive Communion in both kinds), and after the Battle of the White Mountain was presented by Ferdinand II to the Dominicans (1625).

The church was remodelled in Baroque style in 1733. V. V. Reiner was responsible for the ceiling-painting ("Glorification of the Dominican Order") and the altar-piece (St Wenceslas) in the chapel in the north aisle, and was himself buried in the church. The sumptuous confessionals were the work of R. Prachner.

Recitals of Church music are given here from time to time.

St Henry's Church (Kostel svatého Jindřicha)   D5(H10)

Location
Jindřišská ulice (corner of
Jeruzalémská), Nové Město,
Praha 1

Metro
Můstek

Trams
3, 14, 15, 18, 19, 21, 24, 29

This Gothic church was built in 1348–51 as the Parish Church of the New Town, which was founded at the same time. The tower was added in 1475 and originally served as part of the town's defences; it was restored in Gothic style in 1879. In front of the church is a statue of St John of Nepomuk.

The interior was remodelled in Baroque style in the 18th c. On the right of the high altar is a very fine panel-painting of the Virgin. The paintings in the Chapel of the Virgin Dolorosa ("Transfiguration", "Immaculata") are by V. V. Reiner, who ranks with P. J. Brandl as the finest of the fresco-painters of the Bohemian High and Late Baroque.

St Ignatius's Church

See Charles Square

The high altar of St James's Church, with V. V. Reiner's "Martyrdom of St James" ▶

St James's Church (Kostel svatého Jakuba) D5(H9/10)

Location
Malá Štupartská (corner of
Jakubská),
Staré Město, Praha 1

Metro
Můstek

Trams
3, 5, 9, 19, 26, 29

St James's was built in 1232 as the church of the old Minorite
friary (on the north sides). After being destroyed by fire in 1366
it was rebuilt in Gothic style, and was given its present Baroque
form between 1689 and 1739. The stucco front, with figures of
SS. James, Francis and Anthony of Padua, was the work of
Ottavio Mosto.

Interior
St James's is most notable for its interior, with its delicately
modelled pilasters and its 21 altars. It is Prague's longest
church after St Vitus's Cathedral (see Hradčany), and its rich
decoration makes it one of the most beautiful. The "Martyrdom
of St James" on the high altar is by V. V. Reiner, the ceiling-
frescoes ("Life of the Virgin", "Glorification of the Trinity") by
F. Q. Voget. The Baroque monument of Count Vratislav
Mitrovic was designed by Johann Bernhard Fischer von Erlach
and executed by F. M. Brokoff (1714–16).
Since the church has excellent acoustics it is frequently used
for concerts and recitals.
The old Minorite friary on the north side of the church is now
an art school.

St John of Nepomuk (Kostel svatého Jana Nepomuckého) A4

Location
Kanovnická ulice, Nové
Město, Praha 1

Metro
Hradčanská

Trams 22, 23

From Hradčany Square Kanovnická ulice runs north-west to
the Church of St John of Nepomuk, the first church built in
Prague by Kilian Ignaz Dientzenhofer (1720–28). Much of the
tower was destroyed in 1815.
The church has fine ceiling-frescoes by V. V. Reiner ("Glorification of Life", "Miracles of St John of Nepomuk') and altar-
pieces by M. Willmann and J. K. Liška (1701).

St John of Nepomuk on the Rock C7
(Kostel svatého Jana Nepomuckého na skalce)

Location
Vyšehradská 18,
Nové Město, Praha 1

Bus
148

Built by Kilian Ignaz Dientzenhofer in about 1730, this church,
on a centralised plan with twin towers and a double external
staircase, is one of the finest Late Baroque churches in Prague.
The fresco of the Ascension of St John of Nepomuk is by
K. Kovář (1748), the wooden statue of the Saint on the high
altar by Johann Brokoff; a bronze statue based on this model is
on the Charles Bridge (see entry).

St Longinus's Chapel (Rotunda svatého Longina) D6

Location
Na Rybníčku,
Nové Město, Praha 1

Metro
I. P. Pavlova

This round Romanesque chapel was originally a village church,
but the village of Rybníček to which it belonged was absorbed
into the New Town at some time after 1257 and is now recalled
only by the name of the street in which the church stands. Until
the 14th c. it was dedicated to St Stephen.
Notable features of the interior are the Baroque altar and the
representation of the Crucifixion in which Longinus appears.

According to an apocryphal source Longinus was the soldier, or captain, who pierced Christ's side with a lance. Legend has it that he later became a bishop in Cappadocia and suffered a martyr's death.

St Martin's Chapel

See Vyšehrad

St Mary of the Snows (Kostel Panny Marie Sněžné)   D5(G11)

The Church of St Mary of the Snows, the construction of which was ordered by Charles IV in 1347 as a monastic church for the royal coronation, was originally designed to surpass St Vitus's Cathedral in size, but by 1397 only the 30 m (100 ft) high choir had been completed, with the fine Gothic doorway on the north side. In 1611 the vaulting collapsed and was replaced by a Renaissance ceiling. The Baroque high altar (1625–51) is the largest in Prague. Over the left-hand side altar is an "Annunciation" by V. V. Reiner. There is a fine pewter font of 1459.

The church played an important part in the history of the Hussite movement. Here Jan Želivský preached to congregations of the city's poor against the Papal Church, the nobility and the wealthy burghers; and it was Želivský who in 1419 stormed the New Town Hall with the most radical of his

Location
Jungmannovo náměstí,
Staré Město, Praha 1

Metro
Můstek

Trams
5, 9, 19, 29

St Mary of the Snows

supporters and triggered off the Hussite Wars by throwing the Emperor's Catholic councillors out of the window. Even after the murder of Želivský in 1422 St Mary of the Snows remained a centre of the Hussite movement.

Franciscan Garden
(Františkánská zahrada)

The Franciscan Garden on the south side of the church has been a public park since 1950. It is linked by shopping arcades with Wenceslas Square and Vodičkova ulice.

Jungmann Square
(Jungmannovo náměstí)

In Jungmann Square (work on the construction of a Metro station is at present in progress) is the Jungmann Monument (Jungmannův pomník; by L. Šimek). The writer and philologist Josef Jungmann (1773–1847) played a leading part in the rebirth (*obrozeni*) of Czech national consciousness during the Romantic period. He also compiled a large German-Czech dictionary and wrote a history of Czech literature.

St Mary's of Emmaus

See Emmaus Abbey

St Mary the Victorious (Kostel Panny Marie Vítězné)   B5

Location
Karmelitská ulice, Malá Strana, Praha 1

Trams
12, 22

In Karmelitská ulice (Carmelite Street), a short distance west of Maltese Square, stands the Early Baroque Church of St Mary the Victorious, originally a Carmelite church, which was built on the site of an earlier Hussite church after Ferdinand II's victory in the Battle of the White Mountain.

The interior is modelled on the Gesú Church in Rome. On the right-hand wall is the "Christ Child of Prague", a wax figure just under 50 cm (20 in) high, originally from Spain, which Princess Polyxena Lobkowitz presented to the Carmelite friary in 1628 and which is still much revered. In the catacombs under the church are the dried-up bodies – well preserved because of the circulation of air – of Carmelite friars and their benefactors (closed to the public on health grounds).

St Mary under the Chain (Kostel Panny Marie pod řetězem)   B/C5

Location
Lázeňská ulice,
Malá Strana, Praha 1

Trams
12, 22

St Mary under the Chain is the oldest church in the Lesser Quarter (see entry), founded in 1169 together with the house of the Knights of Malta, the administrative centre of the Order in Bohemia. In the right-hand wall of the forecourt can be seen the remains of the original Romanesque church which was burnt down in 1420. The church's two massive towers were completed in 1389. The presbytery was given its present Baroque form by Carlo Lurago in the 17th c.

Notable features of the Baroque interior are the altar-piece on the high altar and a painting of St Barbara, both by Karel Škréta.

St Nicholas's Church in the Lesser Quarter

See Lesser Quarter Square

St Nicholas's Church in the Old Town   D5(G10)
(Kostel svatého Mikuláše)

St Nicholas's, originally the church of a Benedictine house (see Emmaus Abbey), now belongs to the Czechoslovak Hussite Church.

This Baroque church with its monumental south front, long nave with side chapels and dome was built by Kilian Ignaz Dientzenhofer in 1732–35. The sculptural decoration is by Anton Braun, the rich stucco-work by B. Spinetti, the ceiling-paintings ("Lives of St Nicholas and St Benedict") by Peter Asam the Elder. The statue of St Nicholas on the lateral façade is by B. Šimonovský (1906).

After the dissolution of the abbey, the high altar, pews and many of the pictures were removed to other churches.

Adjoining the church, to the left, is the house in which the Prague writer Franz Kafka was born (bust).

Location
Staroměstské náměstí
(Old Town Square),
Staré Město, Praha 1

Metro
Staroměstska

Buses
133, 144, 156, 187

Tram
17

SS. Peter and Paul

See Vyšehrad

St Salvator's Church (Kostel svatého Salvátora)   D4/5(G9)

St Salvator's, originally a German Lutheran church, now belongs to the Bohemian Brethren.

The church was built in Renaissance style in 1611–14 and after being acquired by the Paulian Order was remodelled in Baroque style in 1720 and provided with a tower. The work was financed with the help of contributions from all over Protestant Europe.

Location
Salvátorská,
Staré Město, Praha 1

Metro
Staroměstska

St Salvator's Church in the Clementinum

See Knights of the Cross Square

St Stephen's Church (Kostel Svatého Štěpána)   D6

St Stephen's was founded by Charles IV in 1351 as the Parish Church of the upper New Town and completed in 1394. The tower was added at the beginning of the 15th c. The Gothic exterior of the church has been preserved in spite of restoration work in 1876 and 1936.

Notable features of the church, in addition to the Baroque interior, are the Gothic font (1462), the Gothic Madonna (1472), the Late Gothic stone pulpit, three paintings by Karel Škréta ("St Rosalia", c. 1660, second pier on left; "St Wenceslas", c. 1650, north side of choir; "Baptism of Christ", 1649, end of north aisle) and the monument of the Baroque sculptor M. B. Braun.

Location
Štěpánská ulice,
Nové Město, Praha 1

Metro
I. P. Pavlova

Buses
120, 128, 137, 148, 176

Trams
4, 16, 19, 22, 29

St Thomas's Church (Kostel svatého Tomáše)   B/C4

Location
Letenská ulice, Malá Strana,
Praha 1

Metro
Malostranská

Trams
12, 22

St Thomas's the Gothic origin of which is made evident by the massive buttresses on the outer walls of the presbytery, was founded in 1285 for the Order of Augustinian Hermits and was completed, with the Augustinian friary (now an old people's home) and St Thomas's Brewhouse, in 1379.

The church was remodelled in Baroque style by Karl Ignaz' Dientzenhofer. In a niche over the Renaissance doorway (by Campione de' Bossi, 1617) can be seen a statue of St Augustine by Hieronymus Kohl (1684).

In the richly appointed interior are paintings and statues by Bohemian artists (Karel Škréta, etc.).

St Ursula's Church (Kostel svaté Voršily)   C5/6(F11)

Location
Národni třída 8, Nové Město,
Praha 1

Trams
5, 9, 22, 29

The Baroque Church of St Ursula, with a striking richly articulated façade was built in 1702–04 to the design of Marcantonio Canevale. The statuary group of St John of Nepomuk is by Ignaz Platzer the Elder (1747).

Particularly notable features of the sumptuous Baroque interior are the ceiling-frescoes by J. J. Steinfels, the altar-piece ("Assumption") by Peter Johann Brandl and the statues by F. Preiss.

There is an excellent wine-bar, the Klášterni Vinárna, in the former conventual buildings.

St Vitus's Cathedral

See Hradčany

St Wenceslas's Church in Zderaz   C6
(Kostel svatého Václava na Zderaze)

Location
Resslova ulice, Nové Město,
Praha 1

Buses
120, 128, 134, 137, 176

Trams
3, 17, 21, 27

St Wenceslas's was originally the Parish Church of the commune of Zderaz, which was later incorporated in the New Town. It has belonged to the Czechoslovak Hussite Church since 1926. The present 14th c. Gothic church has preserved some remains of a Romanesque nave and tower. The choir has fragments of Gothic wall-paintings of about 1400. The Late Gothic stellar vaulting dates from 1587.

Facing St Wenceslas's is the Church of SS. Cyril and Methodius (see entry), and Charles Square (see entry) is not far away.

Schönborn Palace (Schönbornsky palác)   B4/5

Location
Tržiště 15, Malá Strana,
Praha 1

Trams
12, 22

This extensive palace, with four wings enclosing a courtyard and a relatively plain façade, is now the United States Embassy. The pediments and dormer windows and the four statues of giants at the entrance to the courtyard were added by Giovanni Santini in about 1715.

The gardens of Schönborn Palace were already widely famed in the mid 17th c. They rise in terraces from the formally patterned flower-beds to the arcaded pavilion (formerly a wine-press) at the top of the hill, from which there is a superb view of Prague.

Schwarzenberg Palace

See Hradčany Square

Šitek Water-Tower (Šitovská věž)   C6

Near the Mánes Exhibition Hall (see entry) is a Renaissance tower, originally dating from the mid 15th c. but much damaged by fire and bombardment and frequently restored. The Baroque roof was added at the end of the 18th c. The tower is named after the owner of the mill (b. 1451). It has supplied the New Town with water since the end of the 15th c.

Location
Gottwaldovo nábřeží 250,
Nové Město, Praha 1

Buses
120. 128, 137, 176, 197

Trams 3, 17

Smetana Embankment (Smetanovo nábřeží)   C5(F10/11)

The Smetana Embankment, named after the composer Bedřich Smetana (see Notable Personalities), extends from the National Theatre to a small peninsula just before the Charles Bridge, offering magnificent views of the Hradčany and Charles Bridge (see these entries).
A path runs along the little peninsula past the Emperor Francis I Monument to the 15th c. water-tower of the Old Town and the Smetana Museum, which has been housed since 1936 in the old Prague Waterworks building, a neo-Renaissance structure of 1883.

Location
Staré Město, Praha 1

Metro
Staroměstská

Tram
17

Spanish Synagogue

See Josefov

Star Castle

See White Mountain

Sternberg Palace

See European Art Collection of the National Gallery

Strahov Abbey and National Literary Memorial   A4/5
(Strahovský klášter, Památník národního písemnictví)

Location
Strahovské nádvoří 132
(entrance also at Pohořelec
8), Hradčany, Praha 1

Trams
22, 23

Opening times
Tues.–Sun. 9 a.m.–5 p.m.

Strahov Abbey, Prague's second oldest religious house, was built in 1143 by Duke Vladislav II, at the request of the Bishop of Olomouc (Olmütz), Jindřich Zdik, for the Premonstratensian Order. Originally situated outside the town, it was brought within the walls by Charles IV. The abbey has been frequently damaged and rebuilt in the course of its history, and the buildings are now predominantly of the 17th and 18th c.
The abbey courtyard can be entered either through a passage at Pohořelec 8 (stairs) or, preferably, by a short steep street at the west end of the square, turning left through a Baroque gateway of 1719.
In the courtyard, on the left, is the old Chapel of St Roch (Kaple svatého Rocha, 1603–11), now the Musaion exhibition hall. Straight ahead is the 17th c. Church of the Assumption (Kostel Nanebevzetí Panny Marie), with a sumptuous Baroque interior (at present in course of restoration: only the high altar is visible).
In the Pappenheim Chapel in the south aisle is the Tomb of Gottfried Heinrich zu Pappenheim (1594–1632), a cavalry general who fell in the Battle of Lützen.
Adjoining the church are the conventual buildings, some of which date from the Romanesque period. Together with the library and the cloister they have housed the National Literary Memorial and the Museum of Czech Literature since 1953.

Strahov Abbey, Prague's second oldest religious house

Philosophical Library, Strahov Abbey

National Literary Memorial

The central element in the Museum of Czech Literature is the old Library of the abbey (reached from the cloister by a staircase leading up to the first floor), which possesses some 900,000 volumes (400,000 outhoused at Kladruby), including about 2500 incunabula, 5000 manuscripts and numerous old maps, making it one of the richest libraries of its kind in the world. Its oldest book is the Strahov Gospel-Book (9th–10th c.; in the corridor between the rooms described below).

The two finest rooms in the Museum are the Theological Library, with rich stucco ornament and paintings of 1723–27 by a Strahov monk, Siard Nosecky, and the Philosophical Library in the neo-Classical west wing (by Ignaz Palliardi, 1782–84). The Philosophical Library's dimensions (32 m (105 ft) long, 10 m (33 ft) wide, 14 m (46 ft) high) were designed to accommodate the richly carved bookcases from Bruch Abbey in Southern Moravia. The huge ceiling-fresco by Franz Anton Maulpertsch of Langenargen (Lake Constance) depicts scenes from the intellectual history of mankind in the allegorical style of the Vienna Academy.

In the cloister and adjoining rooms is Czech literature of pre-Hussite and Hussite times, with particular emphasis on the latter, and also of the period of national revival in the 19th c.

The Museum also contains large stocks of books from many Bohemian religious houses dissolved after the Second World War.

Stromovka Park   D2

Location
U sjezdového paláce,
Holešovice, Praha 7

Trams
2, 13, 17, 24, 29

This beautiful park extends from Letná Hill (see Letná Gardens) to the Vltava. On the south-west side of the park is an old hunting-lodge, originally dating from the 15th c. but rebuilt in neo-Gothic style in 1804, which now houses the newspapers and periodicals department of the National Museum.
At the east end of the park are the Julius Fučík Park of Culture and Recreation (Park kultury a oddechu Julia Fučíka), the Palace of Congresses (Sjezový palać), a sports hall, the Lapidarium of the National Museum and a Planetarium.

Sylva-Taroucca Palace

See Na Příkopě

Theatine Church

See Thun-Hohenstein Palace

Three Ostriches House (U tří pštrosů)   C5

Location
Dražického náměstí 12, Malá
Strana, Praha 1

Metro
Malostranská

Trams
12, 22

This handsome Renaissance house at the Charles Bridge (see entry), built in 1597, preserves remains of painting (by Daniel Alexius Květná, 1606) on its façade. The upper storey, in Early Baroque style, was designed by Caril Geer (1657).
The beamed ceilings in the rooms of the old inn (now a hotel) date from the 17th c.
Prague's first coffee-house was opened here in 1714 by an Armenian named Deodatus Damajan.

Thun-Hohenstein Palace (Thun-Hohenštejnský palác)   B4

Location
Karmelitská ulice 18, Malá
Strana, Praha 1

Metro
Malostranská

Trams
12, 22

This Baroque palace was built by Giovanni Santini in 1710–25 for Norbert Vinzenz Kolowrat. It is now the Italian Embassy.
The palace, which is joined to the Slavata Palace in Thunovská Street, has a magnificent doorway with two heraldic eagles (the device of the Kolowrat family) and figures of Jupiter and Juno.
A short distance away, in the direction of the Hradčany (see entry), is St Cajetan's Church, also known as the Theatine Church, which was built between 1691 and 1717 to the design of Jean-Baptiste Mathey and Giovanni Santini.

*Town Hall of the Old Town (Staroměstská radnice)   D5(G10)

Location
Staroměstské náměstí' (Old
Town Square), Staré Město,
Praha 1

The former Town Hall of the Old Town is now used for cultural and social occasions (e.g. weddings), but has preserved its name as the Town Hall.
The history of the Town Hall, the oldest parts of which date

from the 11th c., is a story of continuing building activity, involving both the conversion of existing burghers' houses and new construction.

In 1338 King John the Blind granted the citizens of the Old Town the right to build their own Town Hall. The nucleus was a house belonging to the Stein family, to which a square tower was added in 1364. The oriel chapel on the north-east side of the tower was consecrated in 1381; it was badly damaged in 1945 but was restored after the war. A casket built into the wall contains earth from the Dukla Pass, where Czech and Russian forces drove back the Germans in 1944. Set into the paving in front of the east side is a stone commemorating the leaders of the Czech Protestant rising, executed in 1621: two white swords, crossed, with the Crown of Thorns, the date of execution and 27 small crosses.

The Astronomical Clock on the south side of the tower was installed at the beginning of the 15th c. The Gothic doorway on the south front, the main entrance, was completed in 1480.

About 1360 the Kříž House was purchased to provide additional accommodation. The inscription over the Renaissance window, "Praga caput regni" (Prague, capital of the kingdom) dates from 1520.

In 1458 a third house was acquired, the Mikeš House, which was rebuilt in neo-Renaissance style in 1878.

In 1830 the House of the Cock (U kohouta) was added to the Town Hall complex. A Romanesque room is still preserved in the basement. Fine Renaissance ceilings and wall-paintings on the first floor.

Building activity did not come to an end until the end of the 19th c. The Town Hall was badly damaged on the last day but one of the Second World War, when the tower was bombarded by the remnants of the Nazi army and the neo-Gothic east and north wings and the municipal archives were destroyed.

The Council Chamber on the second floor has been preserved in its original Gothic form (1470).

In the Great Hall can be seen two pictures by the Czech Historical painter Václav Brožik, "The Election of George of Poděbrad as King of Bohemia" and "Jan Hus before the Council of Constance". In the cloister is the Municipal Gallery. There is a superb panoramic view of Prague from the 70 m (230 ft) high tower (lift).

Adjoining the Town Hall on the south stands the House of the Minute, with sgraffito decoration (Biblical and mythological scenes); originally built about 1600, the house was later remodelled in Renaissance style. The statue of a lion at the corner is 18th c. In the arcading is a passage leading into Little Square (Malé náměstí).

Astronomical Clock (Orloj)

"On this clock were to be seen the course of the heavens throughout the year, with the tale of the months, days and hours, the rising and setting of the stars, the longest and the shortest day, the equinoxes, the feast-days for the whole year, the length of day and night, the new and the full moon with the four quarters, and the three different hours of striking according to the whole and the half hour." So wrote the painter and engraver Matthäus Merian in 1650 about the astronomical clock on the south side of the Town Hall tower; and for the last 500 years hardly anything has changed in the appearance of the clock.

Metro
Staroměstská

Trams
5, 9, 19, 29

Opening times
Mar.–mid Oct., 8 a.m.–6 p.m.; Mid Oct.–Feb., 8 a.m.–5 p.m.

The clock was originally installed in 1410, but in 1490 it was rebuilt by one Master Hanuš of the Charles University. Legend has it that the Municipal Council then had him blinded to prevent him from constructing a similar marvel for any other town. Then, it is said, the blind man climbed the tower shortly before his death and stopped the clock. Thereafter the clock remained silent until Jan Táborský restored the mechanism to working order between 1552 and 1572.

The clock consists of three parts – the procession of Apostles, the face which tells the time and the calendar. The main attraction is the procession of the Apostles, which takes place every hour on the hour. Death, represented by a skeleton, pulls the rope of the funeral bell with one hand and raises his sandglass in the other. The windows open, and Christ and the Twelve Apostles appear. After the windows have closed again a cock flaps his wings and crows, and the clock strikes the hour. Other characters who also feature in the scene are a Turk shaking his head, a miser gloating over his sack of gold and a vain man contemplating his face in a mirror.

The calendar was painted by Josef Mánes. The original is in the staircase hall of the Municipal Museum (see entry).

Troja Palace (Letohrádek Troja)   D1

This handsome Baroque palace, built by Jean-Baptiste Mathey in 1679–85, lies to the north of the Stromovka Gardens (see entry) in the district of Troja, on the far side of the Vltava.

The fine staircase in front of the house was a later addition; its sculptural decoration, depicting a fight between giants and Titans, was the work of Johann Georg Heermann of Dresden and the brothers Johann Josef and Ferdinand Maximilian Brokoff.

A notable feature of the interior is the Imperial Hall, with wall- and ceiling-paintings (1691–97) by the Dutch artist Abraham Godin.

Location
Troja, Praha 7

Bus
112

Opening times
Apr.–Sep., Tues.–Sun.
9 a.m.–5 p.m.

Tuscan Palace (Toskánský palác)   B4

This two-storey palace, with four wings surrounding a courtyard was built by Jean-Baptiste Mathey in 1689–91 for Michael Oswald Thun-Hohenstein. From 1718 to 1918 it belonged to the Dukes of Tuscany.

The harmony of its proportions is enhanced by the way in which it is distanced from its surroundings. The main front has two doorways flanked by columns, the coat of arms of Tuscany above the balconies and a row of Baroque statues on the attic storey.

Location
Hradčanské náměstí 6
(Hradčany Square),
Hradčany, Praha 1

Metro
Hradčanská

Trams
22, 23

◀ *The astronomical clock on the Town Hall*

Tyl Theatre (Tylovo divadlo)   D5(G10)

Location
Železná ulice 11, Staré
Mešto, Praha 1

Metro
Můstek

Trams
5, 9, 19, 29

This neo-Classical building (architect A. Haffenecker), the first theatre in the Vltava Valley, was built for Count Anton von Nostitz-Rieneck in 1781–83. The east front and the interior decoration were the work of Achill Wolf (1881). The Nostitz Theatre was the theatre patronised by the nobility; then in the mid 19th c. it became the German Theatre; in 1945 it was renamed in honour of the Czech dramatist and actor Josef Kajetán Tyl (1808–56), and it is now the second house of the National Theatre.

The triumphant first performance of Mozart's "Don Giovanni" took place in this theatre in 1787. From 1813 to 1816 Carl Maria von Weber was Musical Director here.

*Týn Church (Kostel Panny Marie před Týnem)   D5(G10)

Location
Staroměstské náměstí (Old
Town Square), Staré Město,
Praha 1

Metro
Staroměstská, Můstek

Trams
5, 9, 19, 29

This Gothic church is the landmark and emblem of Prague's Old Town. An aisled church with three presbyteries, it was built in 1365 on the site of an earlier Romanesque church; the choir was completed in 1380; and the façade and the high-pitched roof were built in the reign of George of Poděbrad (1460). The Týn Church was then the principal church of the Utraquists of Bohemia (who believed that the Communion should be administered in both kinds).

George of Poděbrad caused the façade to be adorned with a large gilded chalice (an emblem of the Utraquist doctrine) and

An Old Town landmark: the Týn Church

a statue of himself; but after the defeat of the Protestants in the Battle of the White Mountain (1620) the chalice was replaced by an image of the Virgin.

The 80 m (260 ft) high towers, the spires, of which are surrounded by four elegant little turrets, were built in 1463–66 (the north tower) and 1506–11 (the south tower).
After the great fire of 1679 the nave was given a new Baroque vaulted roof. Note the fine north doorway with its decorated Gothic canopy and tympanum from the workshop of Peter Parler ("Christ's Passion": a copy of the original, which is in the National Gallery's Collection of Bohemian Art in Hradčany Castle (see entry).

Exterior

The interior, with the High Gothic choir and the large Baroque altars, is rather dark.
On the high altar is a fine "Assumption" by Karel Škréta (1610–74).
In the chapel to the left of the choir is a Gothic Pietà.
On the fourth pier to the right of the main entrance can be seen the gravestone of the Danish astronomer Tycho Brahe (1546–1601: see Notable Personalities).

Interior

Týn Court (Týnský dvůr)

D5(G10)

This medieval trading centre (at present in course of renovation), also known as Ungelt (*geld* = "money") after the dues which had to be paid here, was established as early as the 11th c. Within this area, under the protection of the ruling prince – for which they paid a fee – merchants coming to Prague to do business stored, sold and paid customs dues on their wares.
The finest building within the complex is the Granovský Palace, a Renaissance mansion with an open loggia on the first floor (1560) in which visiting merchants could lodge. The wall-paintings in the loggia depict Biblical and mythological scenes.

Location
Staré Město, Praha 1

Metro
Staroměstská, Můstek

Trams
5, 9, 29

Týn School (Týnska škola)

D5(G10)

Originally Gothic, with a rib-vaulted arcade, this building was enlarged in the middle of the 16th c., remodelled in the style of the Venetian Renaissance and given a double pediment.
From the mid 15th c., for 400 years, this was the Tyn parish school.
The Týn Church is through the third arch from the left.

Location
Staroměstské náměstí 14 (Old Town Square), Staré Město, Praha 1

Metro
Staroměstská, Můstek

Trams 5, 9, 19, 29

Tyrš House (Tyršův dům) and Museum of Physical Education and Sport (Muzeum tělesné výchovy a sportu)

B5

The Tyrš House is occupied by the Museum of Physical Education and Sport, with a large collection of material illustrating the development of sport in Czechoslovakia. A special section is devoted to the Sokol gymnastic movement and the Spartakiades (a kind of national equivalent of the Olympic Games).

Location
Újezd 40, Malá Strana, Praha 1

Trams
12, 22

113

Václav Vack Square

Opening times
Museum: Tues.–Sat.
9 a.m.–5 p.m.
Sun. 10 a.m.–5 p.m.

This little Renaissance palace was originally built about 1580. After the Emperor's victory in the Battle of the White Mountain (1620) it was acquired by Pavel Michna Vacinov, who had grown rich from the confiscated property of the rebellious Bohemian nobles, and his son had it remodelled in the style of the Late Renaissance and extended by the addition of an east wing.

From 1767 the mansion was used as an arsenal. After the First World War it was acquired by the Sokol movement and given its present name in honour of the founder of the movement, Miroslav Tyrš.

---

*Václav Vack Square (Náměstí primátora dr. Václava Vacka)   C/D5(G10)

Location
Staré Město, Praha 1

Metro
Staroměstská

This square was formerly known as St Mary's Square after a church dedicated to the Virgin which formerly stood here and played an important part during the German Reformation. As a result of building development in the early 20th c., however, only the south and west sides of the square remain in their original form.

Municipal Library
(Městská lidová knihovna)

Opening times
Tues.–Sun. 10 a.m.–5 p.m.

On the north side of the square stands the Municipal Library, opened in 1928. On the second floor of the library is the National Gallery's Collection of Modern Art (Sbírka moderního umění), mainly consisting of works by 20th c. Czech artists (V. Spálas, J. Zrzavýs, etc.).

The library has over 750,000 volumes as well as a large music collection. In addition to the reading-rooms there are a puppet theatre and a film theatre.

New Town Hall, Václav Vack Square

On the east side of the square is the New Town Hall (1909–12), in a late form of Jugendstil (Art Nouveau), with the office of the Primator (Burgomaster), the council chamber of the National Committee and the offices of the municipal administration.

New Town Hall
(Nová radnice)

At the ends of the façade are statues of the Iron Knight and of Rabbi Löw, who was reputed to have created a golem (man-made human being). At the south-east corner of the square, against the wall of the Clam-Gallas Palace, is a fountain with a figure (by Václav Prachner, 1812) representing the Vltava, familiarly known to the people of Prague as Terezka.

The Clam-Gallas Palace – entrance in Husova třída (Hus Street), which runs south from the square – now houses the Municipal Archives.

Clam-Gallas Palace
(Clam-Gallasův palác)

This magnificent Baroque palace, designed by Viennese architect Johann Bernhard Fischer von Erlach, was built in 1707 for Count Johann Wenzel Gallas. The giants flanking the doorways, the figures on the attic storey and the statue on the fountain in the first courtyard were the work of Matthias Braun. The frescoes on the staircase were painted by Carlo Carlone (1727–30), who was also responsible for the ceiling-paintings in two rooms on the second floor ("Olympus", "Coronation of Art and Learning") and in the library ("Luna, Helios and the Stars").

On the west side of the square is the extensive complex of the Clementinum (see entry).

Valdštejn Palace, Valdštejn Street

See Waldstein Palace, Waldstein Street

The Villa Amerika, home of the Dvořák Museum

Villa Amerika (Letohrádek Amerika) and Dvořák Museum   D7

Location
Ke Karlovu 20, Nové Město,
Praha 2

Metro
I. P. Pavlova

Buses
101, 120, 128, 137, 148,
176

Trams
4, 16, 19, 22, 29

This Baroque mansion was built by Kilian Ignaz Dientzenhofer in 1717–20 as a summer residence for Count Michna (after whom it is also known as the Michna Palace). The richly patterned and finely articulated architecture of the main front make this one of the finest secular buildings of the Baroque period in Prague. The frescoes in the interior are by J. F. Schor (1720). The statuary in the garden came from the workshop of Anton Braun.

The Dvořák Museum now housed in the villa possesses scores and documents relating to the composer, in particular his correspondence with Hans von Bülow and Johannes Brahms. Opening times: Tues.–Sun. 10 a.m.–4 p.m.

Vrtba Palace (Vrtbovský palác)   B5

Location
Karmelitská ulice 25, Malá
Strana, Praha 1

Trams
12, 22

Opening times
Mon.–Fri. 9 a.m.–8 p.m.
Sat. and Sun.
8 a.m.–8 p.m.

The Vrtba Palace was rebuilt in Late Renaissance stye in the 1630s. Its gardens (Vrtbovská zahrada) are among the finest Baroque gardens in Central Europe.

The paintings in the *sala terrena* are by V. V. Reiner. At the entrance to the former vineyard are statues of Bacchus and Ceres by Matthias Braun (c. 1730). On the balustraded double staircase Baroque vases alternate with figures from Greek mythology. From the uppermost terrace there is a superb view of St Nicholas's Church (see Lesser Quarter Square) and the old Town.

Vyšehrad

Location
Praha 1

Metro
Gottwaldova

Buses
134, 138, 148

Trams
3, 17, 21, 27

According to legend the crag of Vyšehrad was the spot where the Princess Libuše or Libussa stood and prophesied the future greatness of Prague and the site of the stronghold of the first Přemyslid rulers (see Quotations – Adalbert Stifter).

The Vyšehrad (High Castle) was probably founded in the 10th c. as the second castle of Prague. The first documentary reference to the castle, however, is in the reign of King Vratislav (1061–92), who transferred his residence from the Hradčany (see entry) to here. In those days the Hradčany was the seat of the bishop. Vratislav built a stone castle and several churches (SS. Peter and Paul, St Lawrence's, etc.) and founded the collegiate chapter, long to be an important centre of culture. The Codex Vyssegradensis, now in the manuscript collection of the Clementinum (see entry), was produced here. The only surviving building of this period is the Round Chapel of St Martin. Soběslav I continued the building activity of his predecessors, but after his death in 1140 the Vyšehrad was neglected in favour of the Hradčany, to which the Bohemian kings now transferred their principal residence.

Charles IV carried out extensive renovation work, surrounding the castle with a circuit of walls which joined up with the town walls. The traditional coronation procession of the Bohemian kings started from the Vyšehrad and proceeded by way of

Palacky Square/Bridge, Emmaus Abbey

Vyšehrad

1 St Martin's Chapel
2 Church of SS. Peter and Paul
3 Cemetery
4 Cemetery arcades
5 Slavín Vault
6 Deanery
7 Foundations of Romanesque Church of St Lawrence
8 Three sculpture groups by J. V. Myslbek
9 Equestrian statue of St Wenceslas by J. G. Bendl (1678. copy)
10 Chotek Gate (1841)
11 St Mary's Chapel
12 Leopold Gate (before 1670)
13 Remains of Late Gothic main gate
14 Tábor Gate (1655–56)

200 m
220 yds

Charles Square, Old Town Square and the Charles Bridge (see entries) to St Vitus's Cathedral in the Hradčany.

During the Hussite Wars, in 1420, almost all the buildings on the Vyšehrad were destroyed, and thereafter craftsmen and tradesmen established the "free town on the Vyšehrad". In the latter part of the 17th c. a Baroque fortress was built on the Vyšehrad. The fortress was dismantled in 1866, and the Vyšehrad cemetery was laid out. Finally in 1911 the fortress was razed to the ground, leaving only the circuit of walls.

The Vyšehrad is at present in course of restoration.

The best plan is to approach the Vyšehrad by Vratislav Steet (Vratislavova) and enter by the Chotek Gate (1841) on the north side. To the right of the gate is a copy of J. G. Bendl's equestrian statue of St Wenceslas (1678).

The street called V pevnosti leads to the oldest building in Prague, the Romanesque Round Chapel of St Martin (Rotunda svatého Martina), which dates from the time of King Vratislav. When the Vyšehrad became a fortress in the 17th c. the chapel was used as a powder-magazine. It was renovated in 1878. The statues by J. V. Myslbek in the adjoining gardens represent figures from Czech legend. From the chapel Štulcova ulice leads to the Deanery, behind which are the foundations of the Romanesque Church of St Lawrence.

St Martin's Chapel

The twin towers of the Church of SS. Peter and Paul, which date only from 1902, have become the principal landmarks of the Vyšehrad. The church itself was built in the second half of the 11th c. It was rebuilt as an aisled basilica in the time of Charles IV, and between 1885 and 1887 was renovated in neo-Gothic style.

Church of SS. Peter and Paul

Notable features of the interior are an 11th c. stone sarcophagus and a 14th c. panel-painting of the "Madonna of Rain" (invoked in time of drought) which is believed to have come from the Emperor Rudolf II's Collection.

117

Church of SS. Peter and Paul

St Martin's Chapel

Cemetery (Vyšehradský hřbitov)	Immediately north of SS. Peter and Paul is the Vyšehrad Cemetery, a national shrine for distinguished representatives of art and culture which was created by the extension of the old medieval churchyard after the fortress was dismantled in 1866. Among those buried in the cemetery and the arcades surrounding it are the composers Smetana and Dvořák and the women writer B. Nemcová. In the Slavín Vault (by Antonin Wiehl and J. Maudr) are buried the sculptor J. V. Myslbek and the violinist Jan Kubelik.
Gates	At the south-east end of the Vyšehrad (fine views) stand the Leopold Gate (Leopoldova brána) and, in a projecting outwork, the Early Baroque Tábor Gate (Táborská brána).

Waldstein Palace (Valdštejnský palác) and Waldstein Gardens   B4
(Zahrada Valdštejnského paláce)

Location Malá Strana, Praha 1	The Waldstein Palace now houses the Ministry of Education and the Komenský Museum, which contains material on the pedagogue and philosopher better known as Comenius (1592–1670). This most sumptuous of Prague's noble residences and its first Baroque palace was built in 1624–30 for Albrecht von Waldstein (Wallenstein), one of the wealthiest nobles of his day, Imperial Generalissimo during the Thirty Years War and later Duke of Friedland (murdered in 1634). Waldstein had 25 houses, three gardens and one of the town gates destroyed in order that he might build his palace facing the Hradčany (see entry). The plans of the palace were drawn
Metro Malostranská	
Trams 12, 22	
Opening times Gardens and Sala Terrena: 9 a.m.– 7 p.m.	

up by Andrea Spezza and Giovanni Pieroni, and the work was carried out under the direction of Giovanni Battista Marini.

In the words of Golo Mann in his "Wallenstein":

"The front is Bohemian Italian, modelled on the Palazzo Farnese . . . The true dimensions of the palace can be grasped only after inspecting the inner courtyards and the park. From the square only the façade can be seen . . .

"The rest – the whole – was no ordinary palace. It was an independent territory, a miniature kingdom amid the huddle of the city, enclosed by subsidiary buildings and a fortress-like park wall. When Wallenstein's carriage rolled into the courtyard to the left of the main front he had everything he needed: a chapel to worship in; a riding-track at the lower end of the park; a bathing grotto with crystals, shells and stalactites; garden walks with statues and fountains."

Waldstein Gardens

The Waldstein Gardens, laid out in Italian Baroque style with grottoes, a pond and an aviary, can be entered from Letenská ulice. Along the walks and on the fountain are copies of bronze statues by the Dutch sculptor Adriaen de Vries, who was then working in Prague; the originals were carried off by the Swedes during the Thirty Years War and are now at Drottningholm Palace, Stockholm. From the gardens there are attractive views of the Hradčany (see entry) and St Vitus's Cathedral. On the west side is the Sala Terrena, designed by Giovanni Pieroni, with frescoes by Baccio del Bianco. Theatrical performances and concerts are given here in summer.

On the north side of the palace is Waldstein Street (see entry).

Waldstein Palace

Waldstein Street (Valdštejnská ulice)   C4

Location
Malá Strana, Praha 1

Metro
Malostranská

Trams
12, 22

Waldstein Street preserves to perfection the style and atmosphere of Baroque Prague. At No. 14, on the left, is the Palffy Palace. At no. 12 is the entrance to the Ledebour Gardens (Ledeburska zahrada), which extend into the gardens of the other palaces in the street and from the steep terraces, with loggias and a pavilion, afford impressive views over the city.
At No. 10 is the Kolovrat Palace (18th c.; now housing part of the Ministry of Culture) and at No. 8 the Fürstenberg Palace (1743–47), now the Polish Embassy (garden not open to the public). Diagonally across the street can be found the former riding school of the Waldstein Palace (Jzdárna Valdštejnského paláce), now used for exhibitions.

Wenceslas Monument (Pomnik svatého Václava)   D6(H11)

Location
Václavské náměstí
(Wenceslas Square), Nové
Město, Praha 1

Metro
Muzeum

Tram
11

In front of the National Museum (see entry), at the south-east end of Wenceslas Square (see entry), is the Wenceslas Monument (by Josef Václav Myslbek, 1912–13).
Wenceslas ruled as Duke of Bohemia from 921 and was murdered by his brother Boleslav in 929 or 935. Following reports of miracles he was canonised and became the Patron Saint of Bohemia (feast day 28 September). Although his murder was in fact an incident in the struggle for power in Bohemia between Saxony and Bavaria, he was honoured as a martyr. Wenceslas (Václav) has long been one of the commonest boys' names in Bohemia.

St Wenceslas, Bohemia's Patron Saint

Wenceslas Square, seen from the National Museum

The statue is surrounded by figures of four other patron saints of Bohemia. In front is St Ludmilla, Wenceslas's grandmother and wife of the first Duke of Bohemia to be baptised. After her murder by pagan opponents she was recognised as Bohemia's first martyr.

Also in front of the statue, on the left, is St Procopius. To the rear are the Blessed Agnes (Anežka) and St Adalbert of Prague (Vojtěch).

There are other statues of St Wenceslas in Knights of the Cross Square (Vintners' Column) and the Vyšehrad (see entries).

---

*Wenceslas Square (Václavské náměstí)   D5/6(G/H10/11)

Wenceslas Square, 680 m (744 yd) long and 60 m (66 yd) wide, is more like a boulevard then a square. It is the centre of modern Prague, surrounded by cinemas, tall office blocks, renowned hotels, restaurants and cafés. With the neighbouring streets (Na Příkopé – see entry, Na Můstku, 28. řijna and Národní) it forms the "Golden Cross", where the commercial and social life of the city has developed most intensively down the centuries.

During the construction of the Metro, Prague's Underground, in recent years the square has been replanned, with particular concern for the interests of pedestrians.

The square was originally laid out in the time of Charles IV as a horse market. It was given its present name in 1848.

At the south-east end of the square is the National Museum, with the Wenceslas Monument (see entries) in front of it.

Location
Nové Město, Praha 1

Metro
Můstek, Muzeum

Trams
3, 5, 9, 14, 15, 18, 19, 21, 24, 29

White Mountain (Bílá Hora) and Star Castle (Letohrádek Hvězda)

Location
Břevnov, Praha 6

Buses
108, 179

Trams
8, 22

This bare limestone hill on the western outskirts of the city, now partly built up, was the scene of the Battle of the White Mountain on 8 November 1620 which decided the destinies of Bohemia under the Habsburgs. Here, in less than an hour, the Protestant nobility's army of mercenaries commanded by Count Matthias von Thun was defeated by the forces of the Catholic League under Maximilian of Bavaria. Elector Frederick of the Palatinate, elected as King of Bohemia by the Estates under a new constitution for an electoral monarchy, was compelled to flee from Prague (the "Winter King", 1619–20), and the country lost its independence, not to be recovered until 1918.

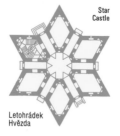

Star Castle

Letohrádek Hvězda

On the north-western slopes of the hill, in a former deer park, is Star Castle.

In 1530 King Ferdinand I established a game park in the Forest of Malejov which later came to be used for royal festivities and marksmanship contests. In 1797 the game park was laid out as an English-style park with broad promenades, called the Star Park (Obora Hvězda) after the old hunting-lodge of that name. The castle lies on the north side of the park's main avenue. This unusual Renaissance building in the form of a six-pointed star, with a completely undecorated exterior, was erected by Italian architects (1555–58) as a hunting-lodge for Ferdinand of Tyrol and became the residence of his future wife Philippine Welser, daughter of an Augsburg patrician. It was later used as a

Star Castle, on the White Mountain

powder-magazine. It now houses a museum devoted to the Czech writer Alois Jirásek and the painter Mikoláš Aleš.
The interior has charming Italian stucco decoration (1556–63), consisting of 334 ceiling-panels with scenes from Greek mythology and Greek and Roman history.

Zoological Garden (Zoologická zahrada)   C1

The Prague Zoo was established in 1931 on 45 hectares (111 acres) of natural country, a mingling of pasture, woodland, hills, rocks and ravines. It now contains more than 2000 animals, representing 600 different species of mammals, fishes and lower forms of life.
The zoo achieved a particular triumph in successfully breeding Przewalski's horse, a wild horse which is now extinct in natural conditions.

Location
Troja, Praha 7

Bus
112

Opening times
Jun.–Aug. 7 a.m.–7 p.m.
May–Sep. 7 a.m.–6 p.m.
Nov.–Feb. 7 a.m.–4 p.m.

Practical Information

It is not always possible to give addresses and/or telephone numbers for all places listed in the Practical Information Section of these guides. This information is readily obtainable from hotel reception desks or from the local tourist office.

Airlines

British Airways
Štěpánská 63, Tel. 24 08 47/8

Czechoslovak Air Lines
(Československé Aerolinie, ČSA)
Revoluční 1, Kotva, Staré Město, Tel. 21 46
Airport: Ruzyně, Tel. 3 34

Lufthansa, Parizska 28, 11000 Praha 1, Tel. 31 75 51

Airport (Letiště)

Prague's international airport is 20 km (12½ miles) north-west of the city centre at Ruzyně. It can be reached by way of Dejvice (Leninova) or Břevnov (Belohorská).

Airport buses depart from and arrive at the ČSA Office, Revoluční 1.

British Airways – Tel. 334 Ext. 4421.
Pan American – Tel. 26 67 47/8 (city).

Extensions are planned for the passenger terminal.

Antiques (Starožitnosti)

Praha 1 (Nové Město), Václavske náměstí 60
Praha 1 (Staré Město), Uhelný trh 6
Praha 1 (Nové Město), Mikulandská 7
Praha 1 (Staré Město), Králodvorská 2
Praha 1 (Staré Město), Můstek 384/3
Praha 2 (Vinohrady), Vinohradská 45
Praha 7 (Holešovice), Šimáčkova 17

Praha 1 (Staré Město), Dažděná 5	Books
Praha 1 (Malá Strana), Mostecká 22	
Praha 1 (Staré Město), Karlova 2	
Praha 1 (Staré Město), Ulice 28. řijna 13	
Praha 2 (Nóve Město), Ječna 36	
Praha 1 (Staré Město), Melantrichova 9	Coins
Praha 1 (Staré Město), Karlova 14	Pictures and graphic art

Art Galleries

Collection of Old Bohemian Art, in St George's Convent
See A to Z – Hradčany

National Gallery collections

Collection of European Art, in Sternberg Palace
See A to Z – Hradčany Square

Collection of 19th-Century Czech Art
See A to Z – St Agnes' Convent

Collection of 20th-Century Czech Art
See A to Z – Václav Vack Square

Collection of Graphic Art, in Kinsky Palace
See A to Z – Kinsky Palace

Collection of 19th and 20th Century Czech Sculpture, in
Zbraslav Palace (10 km (6 miles) from the city centre on the left
bank of the Vltava)
Open Tue.–Sun. 10 a.m.–6 p.m.

Special exhibitions in Belvedere Palace
See A to Z – Belvedere Palace

Exhibitions in Riding-School of Waldstein Palace, Valdštejn-
ská 2, Praha 1
See A to Z – Waldstein Street

Gallery of Central Bohemia (varied collections), Husova 19,
Praha 1 (Old Town)
Open Tue.–Sun. 10 a.m.–6 p.m.

City Gallery, in Old Town Hall
See A to Z – Old Town Hall

Palace of Culture (Palác kultury), Praha 2 (Vyšehrad)
D Gallery, in Portheimka, Matoušova 8, Praha 5 (Smíchov)
Open Tue.–Sun. 10 a.m.–1 p.m. and 2–6 p.m.

Other galleries

Fotochema, Jungmannovo náměstí 18, Praha 1 (New Town)
At present closed

Mánes Exhibition Hall, "Gallery of the Young"
See A to Z – Mánes Exhibition Hall

Banks (Banku)

The country's principal bank is the Československá Státní
Banka (Czechoslovak State Bank).
Praha 1, Na Příkopě 28.
Branches in district (county) towns throughout Czecho-
slovakia.

Czechoslovak State Bank

Monday to Friday 8 a.m. to 3 p.m.

Opening times

Most banks and the most important travel agencies (Čedok,
Pragotur, Autoturist) have an exchange desk where money can

Exchange offices

be changed. At branches of the State Bank foreign currency can be used to buy Tuzex vouchers (see Currency).

Illicit money-changing

Almost all visitors are approached, in their hotel or in the street, by people offering to change money. Deals of this kind are prohibited by law and may attract severe penalties. (Anyone who nevertheless changes money privately should beware of 1000-crown notes, which are no longer current.)

Boat trips on the Vltava

The departure point for passenger boats on the Vltava is at the Palacký Bridge (Palackého most). In addition to short sightseeing cruises, which are a good way of getting a general impression of the city, there are services to various attractive places in the immediate surroundings of Prague, such as Zbraslav or the beautiful Slapy Lake, formed by a dam on the Vltava.

Cafés

City, 1 (Nové Město), Vodičkova 38
Columbia, 1 (Staré Město), Staroměstské náměstí 15
Evropa, 1 (Wenceslas Square), Václavské náměstí 29
Italska cukrárna, 1 (Nové Město), Vodičkova 4
Jahodovy (U Myšáků), 1 (Nové Město), Vodičkova 31
Jalta, 1 (Wenceslas Square), Václavské náměstí 45
Kajetánka, 1 (Hradčany Square), Kajetánské zahrady
Malostranská kavárna, 1 (Malá Strana), Malostranské náměstí 28
Obecnídům, 1 (Staré Město), Náměstí Republiky
Praha, 1 (Wenceslas Square), Václavské náměstí 10
Slavia, 1 (Staré Město), Národní třída 1
Vyšehrad, 2 (Vyšehrad), Palace of Culture (Palác kultury)

Camping sites

Management

Camping sites are run by the Autoturist organisation, Opletalova 29. Places can be reserved by telephone (22 35 44–9).

Camping sites

Kotva
Bránik, U ledáren, Modřanska 55, Tel. 46 17 12
4 km (2½ miles) south of the city centre on the banks of the Vltava

Na Vlachovce
Kobylisy, Rudé armády 217, Tel. 84 12 90
4 km (2½ miles) north of the city centre

Troja
Trojska 131, Tel. 84 28 33
5 km (3 miles) north of the city centre

Caravan
Kbely, Mladoboleslavská 72, Tel. 89 21 14
10 km (6 miles) north-east of the city centre

Sokol Dolní
Počernice, Praha 9, Dolní Počernice, Tel. 71 80 34
6 km (4 miles) east of the city centre

Dolní
Chabry u Prahy
12 km (7½ miles) north of the city centre

Transit
Ruzyně, 25. února 197, Tel. 36 71 08
18 km (11 miles) north-west of the city centre, at the airport
hotel

Caravancamp
Motol, Plzenská, Tel. 52 47 14
5 km (3 miles) west of the city centre

Car rental

PRAGOCAR (also agent for international car rental firms such
as Europcar, Inter-Rent, Godfrey Davis, Avis, etc.):

Praha 1, Štěpánská 42, Tel. 24 00 89, 24 84 85
Ruzyně Airport, Tel. 3 34 42 70, 36 78 07
Inter-Continental Hotel, Tel. 6 43 83

Chemists/Pharmacies (Lekarnu)

Praha 1 (Staré Město), Na Příkopě 7, Tel. 22 00 81   After-hours service
Praha 2 (Nové Město), Ječná 1, Tel. 29 72 90
Praha 6 (Břevnov), Pod Marjánkou 12, Tel. 35 09 67
Praha 10 (Vršovice), Moskevská 41, Tel. 72 44 76

Currency

Czechoslovak currency and the currencies of other Eastern
Bloc States may not be brought into or taken out of
Czechoslovakia. Other currencies may be imported or exported
without limitation and without any declaration.

Import and export of currency

The unit of currency is the Czechoslovakian crown (koruna,
abbreviated Kčs), which is divided into 100 heller (haléř,
abbreviated hal). There are banknotes for 10, 20, 50, 100 and
500 crowns (the 1000-crown notes are no longer current) and
coins in denominations of 1, 2 and 5 crowns and 5, 10, 20 and
50 heller.

Czechoslovak currency

Visitors to Czechoslovakia are granted a 75 per cent bonus over
the official rate of exchange. This tourist rate is at present about
15 Kčs to the £ sterling, 9·5 to the US$. In addition visitors
booking an inclusive tour through Čedok (see Information) can
buy currency vouchers entitling them to a further bonus of 36 per
cent over the tourist rate. The vouchers can be cashed only at
Čedok Interhotels and Čedok offices dealing with tourists. All
currency obtained under this special bonus arrangement must be
spent in Czechoslovakia and is not re-exchangeable or
refundable.

Exchange rate

Visitors can obtain Tuzex vouchers, which are required, as an alternative to hard currency, for purchases in Tuzex shops (see Shopping). These vouchers can be obtained, at the official (not the tourist) rate of exchange, from Tuzex, Alimex or exchange offices (see Banks).

Money can be changed at the tourist rate only in the exchange offices of the State Bank (see Banks), Interhotels and leading travel agencies and at frontier crossing-points.

Private or black market exchange transactions should be avoided: they are illegal and subject to severe penalties.

Obligatory minimum exchange

All foreign visitors are required to spend at least £8 $12 (children aged 7 to 15 half as much: both figures subject to change) per person per day while in Czechoslovakia. Visitors who have reserved and prepaid hotel accommodation or other services, and those who have bought Čedok currency vouchers if no services have been prearranged, are exempt from this requirement. Unspent local currency over the obligatory minimum may be reconverted at official exchange offices when leaving Czechoslovakia (except if travelling by train).

Credit cards

The following credit cards are accepted by Čedok, hotels, Tuzex shops and certain other shops and restaurants: Diners Club, Access, Visa, American Express.

Customs regulations

Import

Personal effects which are necessary for use during the visit (clothing, personal jewellery, sports equipment, cameras and ciné (movie) cameras, portable typewriters, tape recorders, transistor radios, etc.) may be taken into Czechoslovakia duty-free. There are also duty-free allowances of 250 cigarettes (or the equivalent in other forms of tobacco), 2 litres of wine, 1 litre of spirits, $\frac{1}{2}$ litre of eau-de-Cologne or toilet water, 3 kilograms of foodstuffs and gifts to the value of Kčs 600. The import of pure spirit is prohibited.

All objects of value must be entered in the foreign currency certificate (page 3 of visa application) and must be produced on leaving Czechoslovakia. No personal effects may be disposed of or gifted in Czechoslovakia except on payment of the appropriate customs dues.

Export

Gifts and souvenirs to the value of Kčs 600, and goods bought in Tuzex shops, may be exported without payment of duty. Antiques may be exported only if bought in Tuzex or specially appointed shops. Crystal not bought in Tuzex shops may be subject to duty of up to 100 per cent.

Petrol station receipts

It is advisable to keep receipts for petrol (particularly diesel fuel) until leaving the country.

Department stores

Prior Kotva, Praha 1, náměstí Republiky 8
One of the largest and most modern department stores in Eastern Europe, with a restaurant and snack-bar.
Textiles, foodstuffs, household articles, stationery, etc.; services.

Kotva, Prague's largest department store

Bilá labuť (White Swan), Praha 1, Na poříčí 23
A general department store with a range of goods second only
to Kotva.

Prior Maj, Praha 1, Národni 26
Clothing, footwear, foodstuffs, industrial products; refresh-
ment rooms; services

Prior Dětsky dům, Praha 1, Na Příkopě 15
Children's store.

Družba, Praha 1, Václavské náměstí 21
China, leather goods, clothing, furniture, jewellery. Restaurant
and café with outlook terrace.

Dům potravin, Praha 1, Václavské náměstí 59
Foodstuffs.

Dům obuvi, Praha 1, Václavské náměstí 6
Footwear.

Dům mody, Praha 1, Václavské náměstí 58
"Fashion House"

Dům kožešin, Praha 1, Železná 14
Furs

Dům sportu, Praha 1, Jungmannova 28
Sports goods

Dům hudebních nástrojů, Praha 1, Jungmannovo náměstí 17
Musical instruments.

131

Electricity

220 volts AC; in some of the older parts of the city still 120 volts AC. A universal adaptor should be taken for electric razors, etc.

Embassies

United Kingdom
Thunovská 14, Praha 1,
Tel. 53 33 47–9, 53 33 40, 53 33 70

United States
Tržiště 15, Praha 1,
Tel. 53 66 41–8

Canada
Mickiewiczova 6, Praha 6,
Tel. 32 69 41

Emergencies

Medical emergency service
Visitors can obtain physical examination and treatment at outpatient departments and polyclinics in the district in which they are staying.

Doctor on duty
Dial 155

Ambulance
Dial 333

Dental emergency service
Vladislavova 22, Praha 1, Tel. 26 13 74
Mon.–Fri. 7 p.m.–7 a.m., Sat. and Sun. day and night

Pharmacist on duty
Na Příkopé 7, Praha 1, Tel. 22 00 81

Events

February
Matthias Fair in Julius Fučík Park of Culture and Recreation

April
Intercamera (International Exhibition of Audio-Visual Technology)

May–June
Prague Spring Festival

Peace Run (international cycle run from Prague to Berlin and Warsaw)

June
International Television Festival

Memorial ceremonies in Lidice

October
International Jazz Festival

Excursions

See Sightseeing

Food and drink

Bohemian cuisine is famed for its tasty and substantial dishes and its variety of farinaceous foods (dumplings, pancakes).

The most popular meat dishes are boiled or roast pork, served with cabbage and dumplings, poultry of all kinds, fried sausage, Prague ham and Prague sausages. Another excellent dish is roast loin of beef or venison in cream sauce.

Meat dishes

Vegetables are not a great Prague speciality. Those who want fresh vitamins should ask for lettuce, cucumber, tomato or mixed salad according to season.

Vegetables

Dumplings, in soup or as an accompaniment to meat, are made from flour, bread or potatoes, and may have a bacon filling. Better known, however, are the sweet dumplings, made with fruit (cherries, apricots, plums).

Dumplings

Prague pancakes, more substantial than the *crêpes* of Brittany and filled with curd or cottage cheese, jam or chocolate, are extremely appetising.

Pancakes

		A brief guide to the menu
bažant s červeným zelím a bramborovým knedlíkem	pheasant with red cabbage and potato dumplings	
candát po mlynářsku s hranolky	pike-perch meunière with fried potatoes	
husa s knedlíkem a zelím	goose with dumplings and cabbage	
husí drůbky s rýží	goose giblets with rice	
jablkový koláč	apple cake	
jablkový závin	apple strudel	
kachna se zelím a knedlíkem	duck with cabbage and bread dumplings	
kapr na modro s bramborem	carp au bleu with boiled potatoes	
koroptev s červeným zelím	partridge with red cabbage	
merunkové knedlíky	apricot dumplings	
olomoucké syrečky	Olomouc sour milk cheese	
ovar s křenem a chlebem	boiled pork with horse-radish and bread	
palačinky s tvarohem	pancakes with curd cheese	
pečená štika	roast pike	
pečené kuře s bramborovou kaší	roast chicken with potato purée	
pražský řízek s chřestem	Prague schnitzel with asparagus and potatoes	
pstruh na másle	trout in melted butter	
smažený kapr s míchaným salátem	fried carp with mixed salad	
špekové/chlupaté/knedlílky se zelím	bacon dumplings with cabbage	
srnčí kýta s kroketami a brusinkami	haunch of venison with croquettes and cranberries	

šunka s oblohou	Prague ham, garnished
svestkové knedlíky s tvarohem a máslem	plum dumplings with curd cheese and butter
svíčková na smetaně	roast loin of beef with cream sauce
uzené s okurkou a chlebem	smoked meat with gherkins and bread
vdolky, lívance	pancakes
vepřové se zelím	roast pork with sauerkraut
vídeňský řízek s bramborovym salátem	Wiener schnitzel with potato salad
zajačí hřbet na smetaně	hare in cream sauce

Beer

Beer comes in varying strengths, the main types being light (světlé pivo), lager (ležák), dark (tmavé pivo) and strong dark (silne černé). The best is the widely exported Pilsner Urquell (Plzeňský Prazdroj, 12 per cent), but no less famed are Budweiser (Budvar), the dark Flek beer (U Fleků), the locally brewed beers of Smíchov (Staropramen), Braník (Spezial) and Holešovice (Pragžanka), Pilsner Gambrinus and other well-chilled beers served in the Prague beer-halls. By way of appetisers to accompany the beer there are salted and smoked meats, curd cheese, garlic bread and potato fritters.

Wine

The wine-houses of Prague sell some of the internationally known wines, but the most popular are the Czech wines including Melnik Ludmila, Žernosecke, Velkopavlické, Valtické and Primatorské.

Spirits

"Hard" spirits of Czech origin are slivovice (plum brandy), meruňkovice (apricot brandy), žitná or režná (corn schnapps) and jalovcová or borovička (types of gin). To cure a stomach disorder the Becherovka of Karlovy Vary (Karlsbad), a herb liquor, is recommended.

Soft drinks

Coffee is normally Turkish coffee, boiled and served with the grounds. Italian-style espresso coffee can be had, but must be specially asked for. Viennese coffee, with half a glassful of whipped cream, can also be had.
Also available are tea (čaj), milk (mléko) and fruit juice (orange, grapefruit).

Getting to Prague

By car

The distance from the Channel to Prague is between 965 and 1130 km (600 and 700 miles). Perhaps the best route is to follow E 5, which runs from Ostend to Nuremberg, and then switch to E 12, crossing into Czechoslovakia at Waidhaus/Rozvadov.

Other frontier crossings are:
from West Germany   Schirnding/Pomezí
Furth im Wald/Folmava
Bayerisch Eisenstein/Železná Ruda
Philippsreuth/Strážný

from Austria	Wullowitz/Dolní Dvořiště
	Gmünd/České Velenice
	Haugsdorf/Hatě
	Drasenhofen/Mikulov
	Berg/Petržalka
	Grametten/Nová Bystřice
	Laa an der Thaya/Hevlin
	Weigetschlag/Stúdanky
	Neu-Hagelberg/Halámky
	Hainburg/Bratislava

The distance to Prague from the German border ranges between 160 and 200 km (100 and 125 miles), from the Austrian border between 170 and 400 km (105 and 250 miles). On all these roads there is likely to be much heavy goods traffic. Most of the Czech motorways are still under construction, and only certain stretches are open to traffic.

In addition to the normal travel documents (see entry), motorists should have their national driving licence or (preferably) an international driving licence, the car's registration document and a "green card" (international insurance certificate). If you are driving someone else's car you must be able to produce his written authority. The car must have an oval nationality plaque. If the car shows signs of damage a certificate to that effect must be obtained at the frontier.

All accidents within Czechoslovakia, even if the damage is trivial, must be reported to the police.

Fill up with super grade petrol (not available at all pumps) to avoid knocking.

Petrol coupons offering a 20 per cent reduction on petrol prices can be obtained from Čedok (see Information) or at frontier crossing-points. If you are entitled to the currency bonus (see entry), however, the saving is less advantageous.

There are regular services by Czechoslovak buses from Frankfurt, Munich and Vienna to Prague, arriving at Florenc bus station on Vitězného Února. **By bus**

From Britain the most convenient services are via Paris from where there is a daily through train to Prague or via Cologne from where through carriages convey passengers to the Czechoslovakian capital. There are also good services to Prague from Frankfurt am Main, Nuremberg and Stuttgart, as well as from Zürich (with a change), Berlin and Vienna. From Frankfurt the journey takes 11 hours, from Zürich 14–18 hours, from Vienna 8 hours. Seat reservation is advisable. There are some night services with sleepers. **By rail**

Trains arrive at Prague's Central Station at Ulice Vitězného února 16, which since its reconstruction in 1970 has had one of the most modern passenger concourses in Europe. The Hlavní nádraží Metro Station is at this station.

There are direct flights from London to Prague by British Airways and Czechoslovakian State Airlines (ČSA). There are weekly direct flights from New York to Prague by ČSA, and Lufthansa has frequent services via Frankfurt. **By air**

Practical Information

Prague Airport at Ruzyně is 20 km (12½ miles) north-west of the city on the road to Kladno. There is a bus service from the airport to the city centre and the journey takes about an hour. There are also taxis and car rental facilities.
Czechoslovak Air Lines can arrange accommodation in Prague.

Hospitals

Prague has some 20 hospitals and a home for the care of infants.
For foreigners living in the city centre treatment is provided by the Health Institute at Palackého 5, Praha 1.
Outpatient care for foreigners is provided by the District Outpatient Department (OÚNZ) for the area in which they are staying.
In a case of medical emergency dial 155.
See Emergencies

Hotels

Reservations

Advance reservation of rooms is necessary.

Categories

Hotels are divided into five categories: A* de luxe, A*, B*, B and C.
A* de luxe, A* and some B* hotels are classed as Interhotels. In these hotels visitors can look for excellent accommodation (private bath or shower; suites) and staff who can speak their language. They usually have exchange offices, souvenir shops, bars and several restaurants.
Category B* can be classed as very good, category B as good. Category C applies to more modest hotels. These hotels are not handled by Čedok, but rooms can be booked either through the ČKM-SSM Youth Travel Agency or directly at reception.

Category A* de luxe

Alcron, Praha 1, Štěpánská 40, Tel. 24 57 41
Esplanade, Praha 1, Washingtonova 19, Tel. 22 25 52
Intercontinental, Praha 1, náměstí Curieových, Tel. 28 99
International, Praha 6, náměstí Družby 1801/1, Tel. 32 10 51
Jalta, Praha 1, Václavské náměstí 45, Tel. 26 55 41

Category A*

Ambassador, Praha 1, Václavské náměstí 5, Tel. 22 13 51 or 22 67 45
Olympik I, Praha 8, Invalidovna, Sokolovska tr. 138, Tel. 82 87 41
Panorama, Praha 4, Milevská 7, Tel. 74 93 41
Park, Praha 7, Veletržni 20, Tel. 38 07 01 11

Category B*

Ametyst, Praha 2, Makarenkova 11, Tel. 25 92 56–59
Axa, Praha 1, Na poříčí 40, Tel. 24 95 57
Belvedere, Praha 7, Třída Obránců míru 19, Tel. 37 47 41
Beránek, Praha 2, Bělehradská 110, Tel. 25 45 44
Central, Praha 1, Rybná 8, Tel. 6 40 54
Centrum, Praha 1, Na poříčí 31, Tel. 6 40 54
Družba, Praha 1, Václavské náměstí 16, Tel. 24 05 16
Evropa, Praha 1, Václavské náměstí 29, Tel. 26 39 05
Flora, Praha 3, Vinohradská 121, Tel. 27 42 41

The Intercontinental, one of Prague's luxury hotels

Olympik II (no rest.), Praha 8, Invalidovna, Tel. 83 47 41
Palace, Praha 1, Panská 12, Tel. 26 83 41
Pariz, Praha 1, U Obecního domu 1, Tel. 6 72 51
Splendid, Overnecká 33, Tel. 37 54 51
Tatran, Praha 1, Václavské náměstí 22, Tel. 24 05 41
Vitkov, Praha 3, Koněvova 114, Tel. 27 93 41
Botes (Hotels on Boats), category HB*
Admiral, Praha 5, Hořejší nábřeží, Tel. 54 74 45–49

Albatros, Praha 1, nábřeží Ludvíka Svobody, Tel. 6 00 67   Category B
Adria, Praha 1, Václavské náměstí 26, Tel. 24 86 22
Atlantic, Praha 1, Na poříčí 9, Tel. 6 55 56, 6 36 04
Erko, Praha 9, Kbely 723, Tel. 89 21 05
Hybernia, Praha 1, Hybernská 24, Tel. 22 04 31
Junior, Praha 2, Žitná 12, Tel. 29 99 41
Juventus, Praha 2, Blanická 10, Tel. 25 51 51
Koruna, Praha 1, Opatovická 16, Tel. 29 39 33
Kriván, Praha 2, Náměstí I.P. Pavlova 5, Tel. 29 33 41–44
Lunik, Praha 2, Londýnská 50, Tel. 25 27 01
Merkur, Praha 1, Těšnov 9, Tel. 6 96 56
Meteor, Praha 1, Hybernská 6, Tel. 22 92 41, 22 42 02
Michle, Praha 4, Nuselská 124, Tel. 42 71 17
Modrá Hvězda, Praha 9, Jandova 3, Tel. 93 02 91
Moráň, Praha 2, Na Moráňi 15, Tel. 29 42 53, 29 42 51
Opera, Praha 1, Těšnov 13, Tel. 6 29 44
Praga, Praha 5, Plzeňská 29, Tel. 54 87 41
Racek, Praha 4, Dvorecká Louka, Tel. 42 60 51, 57, 93
Savoy, Praha 1, Keplerova 6, Tel. 53 80 15
Transit, Praha 6, Ruzyně, 25. února 197, Tel. 36 71 08

Practical Information

U tří pštrosů, Praha 1, Malá Strana, Dražického náměstí 12, Tel. 53 61 51
Union, Praha 2, Jaromírova 1, Tel. 43 78 58
Vltava, Praha 5, Zbraslav II, Žitavského 115, Tel. 59 15 49
Zlatá Husa, Praha 1, Václavské náměstí 5, Tel. 22 13 51

Category C

Balkan, Praha 5, Třída svornosti 28, Tel. 54 07 77
Hvězda, Praha 6, Na rovni 34, Tel. 36 89 65, 36 80 37
Moravan, Praha 7, Dimitrovo náměstí 22, Tel. 80 29 05
Na Kopečku, Praha 4, Modřanská 199, Tel. 46 05 38
Stará Zbrojnice, Praha 1, Všehrdova 16, Tel. 53 28 15
Tichý, Praha 3, Kalininova 65, Tel. 27 30 79

Information

In the United Kingdom

Čedok (Czechoslovak State Travel Bureau),
17–18 Old Bond Street,
London W1X 4RB
Tel. 01–629 6058

In the United States

Čedok,
10 East 40th Street,
New York NY 10016
Tel. (212) 689 9720

In Prague

Čedok,
Praha 1, Na Příkopě 18, Tel. 22 42 51–59
Pražska informačni služba (Prague Information Service),
Praha 1, Na Příkopě 20, Tel. 54 44 44

The Prague Information Service publishes "A Month in Prague", with information about events in Prague during the current month. It also produces a 12-page brochure with the programmes of all theatres and cinemas and information about concerts and exhibitions.

Other Čedok offices

Ruzyné Airport, Tel. 36 78 02–03
Hotel Panorama, Milevská ulice 7, Tel. 41 68 58

Čedok provides not only all the information visitors will require but a variety of other services. It will obtain tickets for theatres, concerts and other events, admission to night-spots, air or rail tickets, seat reservations, shooting or fishing permits, etc.; it will arrange car hire, advise on the best garages to repair your car and change travellers' cheques; and it organises city tours and coach excursions (see Sightseeing).

Room booking service

Čedok, Praha 1, Panská 5, Tel. 22 56 57, 22 70 04

City guides

Pragtour, Praha 1, U Obecního domu 2
Private guides can be hired through PIS at Panská 4,
Tel. 22 34 11, 22 43 11, 22 60 67

Directory service

To inquire about someone's address, apply to:
Ustřední evidence obyvatelstva,
Praha 1, Celetná 31
(Apply either in writing or in person; telephone inquiries are not dealt with. Charge 5 Kčs).

Language

It is not necessary to know any Czech to go to Prague. The staff of hotels, travel agencies, etc., with whom visitors will be in contact will speak some English, and young people tend to know English or French; older people may still speak some German.

It is an advantage, however, to have a few words of Czech. The pronunciation is not difficult, though the diacritic marks make it look rather fearsome.

The stress is almost invariably on the first syllable of a word: remember that the semi-vowels *l* and *r* may also carry the accent.

Vowels may be either short or long. A long vowel is indicated by an accent (or in the case of *u* by a small circle). The *e* with a reverse circumflex accent (*ě*) is pronounced *ye*.

The vowels are pronounced in the continental fashion, without the diphthongisation found in English. Consonants are much as in English, with the following special cases:

c	= ts	ř	= rzh as in surgeon
č	= ch as in church	š	= sh as in shush
ch	= ch as in loch	ž	= zh as in treasure
ň	= ny as in canyon	dž	= j as in judge

address	adresa	luggage	zavazadlo	Some useful words
bank	banku	name	jméno	
bill	účet	no	ne	
bread	chléb	pay (verb)	platiti	
chemist's shop	lékárna	please	prosím	
doctor	lékař	post office	pošta	
English	anglický	railway station	nádraží	
good	dobrý	thank you	děkuji	
help	pomoc	without	bez	
I	ja	yes	ano	
lavatory	záchod			

hill	hora	square	náměstí	Topographical terms
chapel	kaple	palace	palác	
church	kostel	street	třída, ulice	
bridge	most	tower	věž	
embankment	nábřeží			

1 jeden	4 čtyři	7 sedm	10 deset	Numbers
2 dva	5 pět	8 osm	20 dvacet	
3 tři	6 šest	9 devět	100 sto	

Libraries

The State Library of the ČSSR comprises the following separate libraries:

University Library
National Library
Slav Library
State Library of Technology
See A to Z – Clementinum

Library of the National Museum
See A to Z – National Museum

Library of Art History and Applied Art
See A to Z – Museum of Applied Art

National Literary Memorial and Museum of Czech Literature
See Strahov Abbey

Lost property offices

Documents   Praha 1, Bartolomějská 14, Tel. 21 49

Other objects   Praha 1, Staré Město, Kaprová 14, Tel. 6 01 44

Motoring

General

Traffic regulations are much the same in Czechoslovakia as in other European countries. Vehicles travel on the right, with overtaking (passing) on the left. The penalties for traffic offences are high.
Safety-belts must be worn. Driving after taking alcohol is absolutely prohibited.
It is permissible to give a lift to a hitch-hiker. Hitch-hiking is prohibited only on motorways.

Speed limits

On motorways: 110 km p.h. (68 m.p.h.)
Outside built-up areas: 80 km p.h. (50 m.p.h.)
Inside built-up areas: during the day 60 km p.h. (37 m.p.h.), at night (11 p.m. to 5 a.m.) 90 km p.h. (56 m.p.h.)
Within 30 m (33 yd of a level crossing: 30 km p.h. ($18\frac{1}{2}$ m.p.h.)

Petrol stations

The following petrol stations selling super grade petrol are always open:
Praha 3 (Žižkov), Kalšnická
Praha 3 (Žižkov), Olšanská
Praha 4 (Újezd, Průhonice), on E 14 (motorway to Brno)
Praha 5 (Motol), Plzenská-Podháj
Praha 6 (Vokovice), Leninova (direction of airport)
Praha 8 (Karlín), Karlínské náměstí
Praha 9 (Hrdlöřezy), Českobrodská
Praha 9 (Prosek)

Parking

Motorists in Prague have the choice between leaving their car in one of the city's large car parks or subjecting themselves to the frustrations of driving in the city. Since the movement of traffic is blocked by the frequent road works in the city centre there are constant traffic jams, delays and diversions (indicated by a blue sign with a yellow arrow and the legend "Objížďka", also in yellow).
Parking in "no parking" areas should be avoided. The police are tough with offenders – even with foreigners – and are quick to tow away vehicles parked in the wrong place. The pound for cars so removed is in Černokostelecká Street, Praha 10 (Hostivař), Tel. 6 01 44. The charge for releasing an impounded vehicle is considerable.

Visitors arriving by car should ask at the frontier for a list of the telephone numbers of the breakdown service (Silniční Služba), the "Yellow Angels", whose patrols operate on all main roads in Czechoslovakia and in case of emergency can be summoned by telephone. In Prague itself breakdown assistance and tow-away service can be called at 22 49 06 and 22 35 44–9.

The Autoturist office at Opletalova 29, Praha 1, Tel. 23 35 44–9, supplies information and advice, issues up-to-date information about road conditions (road maps, town plans), and can arrange accommodation in hotels and motels and on camping sites.

Tel. 24 24 24.

Praha 4 (Spořílov), Severní XI, Tel. 76 67 51–53; reception, Tel. 22 61 96.

Praha 1 (Nové Město), Opletalova 9;
Sales office, Václavské náměstí 18, Tel. 29 05 13.

Museums

Alois Jirásek and Mikoláš Aleš Museum
See A to Z – White Mountain, Star Castle

Anthropological Museum
Praha 2 (Nové Město), Viničná 7
Open only by telephone appointment

Dvořák Museum
Praha 2 (Nové Město), Ke Karlovu 20
Open Tues.–Sun. 10 a.m.–4 p.m.

Ethnographic Museum
See A to Z

Gottwald Museum
Praha 1 (Staré Město), Rytířská 29
Open Tue.–Sat. 9 a.m.–5 p.m., Sun. 9 a.m.–3 p.m.

Historical Museum
See A to Z – National Museum

Jewish Museum
See A to Z – Josefov

Komenský Museum
See A to Z – Waldstein Palace

Lenin Museum
Praha 1 (Nové Město), Hybernská 7
Open Tue.–Sat. 9 a.m.–5 p.m., Sun. 9 a.m.–3 p.m.

Military Museum of the Czechoslovak Army
Praha 3 (Žižkov), U Památníku 2

Mozart Museum
See A to Z – Bertramka

Façade of the Gottwald Museum

The decorated gable of the Smetana Museum

Municipal Museum
See A to Z

Museum of Applied Art
See A to Z

Museum of Central Bohemia
Roztoky u Prahy
Open daily 9 a.m.–6 p.m.

Museum of Czech Literature
See A to Z – Strahov Abbey

Museum of Military History
See A to Z – Hradčany Square, Schwarzenberg Palace

Museum of Natural History
See A to Z – National Museum

Mueum of Physical Education and Sport
See A to Z – Tyrš House

Museum of Postal and Telecommunications Services
Praha 5 (Smíchov), Holeckova 10
Open Mon.–Fri. 9 a.m.–3 p.m.

Music Mueum
Praha 1 (Malá Strana), Lázeňská 2
Open Tues.–Sun. 10 a.m.–5 p.m.

Náprstek Museum (Ethnological Collection)
Praha 1 (Staré Město), Betlémské náměstí 1
Open Tues.–Sun. 9 a.m.–5 p.m.

National Museum
See A to Z

National Museum of Technology
See A to Z

Smetana Museum
Praha 1 (Staré Město), Novotného lávka 1
Open Wed.–Mon. 10 a.m.–5 p.m.

Music

National Theatre (Národní divadlo)   Opera and ballet
Praha 1 (New Town), Národní třída 2
Opera

Smetana Theatre (Smetanovo divadlo)
Praha 1 (New Town), Vítězného února 6
Opera and ballet

Tyl Theatre (Tylovo divadlo)
Praha 1 (Old Town), Železná ulice 11
Opera and drama

Practical Information

Music Theatre (Divadlo hudby)
Praha 1 (New Town), Opletalova 5
Opera, ballet, operettas
(Large exhibition hall and extensive collection of recordings)

Operettas and musicals

Karlin Music Theatre (Hudební divadlo v Karlině)
Praha 8 (Karlin), Krizikova 10

Nusle Music Theatre (Hudební divadlo v Nuslich)
Praha 4 (Nusle), Křesomyslova 625

Musical cabaret

Rococo Theatre (Divadlo Rokoko)
Praha 1 (New Town), Václavské náměstí 38

Poetry and jazz

Viola
Praha 1 (Old Town), Národní třída 7
"Poetry wine-bar", with readings by poets, jazz groups

Concerts and recitals in churches

With their excellent acoustics, Prague's churches are frequently used for concerts and recitals: St Vitus's Cathedral (see Hradčany), St Nicholas's (see Lesser Quarter Square), St James's, etc.

Prague Spring

The Prague Spring Musical Festival, held in June, has established an international reputation. During the festival concerts are given in the Palace of Culture, in churches and in various historical buildings.

Summer concerts

During the summer there are concerts in the Hradčany Gardens.

Opera in the Smetana Theatre

Opening times

Most food shops open at 8 a.m., other shops usually at 9, and close at 6 p.m. (on Saturday at noon). Some of the large department stores stay open until 7 p.m.

Shops

Open Mon.–Fri. 8 a.m.–3 p.m.

Banks

Open Mon.–Fri. 8.30 a.m.–5 p.m.

Public offices

Open Tues.–Sun. from 10 a.m.

Galleries

Open Tues.–Sun. from 9 a.m. (but for the opening times of the various museums see A to Z, also Museums). The Jewish Museum is closed on Saturday but open on Monday.

Museums

Open Apr.–Sept. from 8 a.m. (closed for an hour at lunchtime), Oct.–Mar. from 9 a.m. (not closed at lunchtime)

Castles and palaces

Open until 2 p.m. on Saturdays, June–Sept.

Čedok offices

Police

Police station (People's Police, Veřejná bezpečnost):
Praha 1 (Staré Město), Konviktská 14, Tel. 21 21, 21 49

Service always available in an emergency: Tel. 24 24 24

Emergency service

Dial 158

Emergency calls

Postal services

Praha 1, Jindřišská 14, Tel. 26 48 41
Open 24 hours a day

Head Post Office

Within the ČSSR:
letter (dopis) 1 Kčs, postcard (dopisnice) 0.50 Kčs
To the United Kingdom: letter 4–7 Kčs, postcard 4 Kčs
To the United States or Canada: letter 9–18 Kčs, postcard 9 Kčs
Additional charges for registered (doporučeňe) and express (expres) mail
The word for stamp is *znamka*.

Postage rates

Charged per word (minimum 7 words)

Telegrams

Public holidays and commemoration days

January 1 (New Year's Day), Easter Monday, May 1 (Labour Day), May 9 (National Day), December 25 and 26 (Christmas)

Official public holidays

August 29 (Slovak national rising)
October 28 (declaration of independence and nationalisation of industry)

Commemoration days
(working days)

Public transport

Trams, buses and trolleybuses

Flat-rate fare 1 Kčs (direct journey without changing). Tickets can be bought in hotels and railway stations, at newspaper and tobacco kiosks and at transport offices.
Tickets must be bought in advance and must be punched by the passenger in the cancelling machine on entering the vehicle. There are no conductors.
On the principal routes there are frequent services throughout the day (during the night at intervals of about 40 minutes).

Underground (Metro)

The Metro runs from 5 a.m. to midnight. There are no tickets: the passenger operates the turnstile at the entrance by putting in a 1 Kčs coin.

Railway stations

Prague has some 40 railway stations. Trains from West Germany and Austria arrive at the Central Station, trains from Berlin at the Střed Station.

Central Station (Hlavní nádraží)
Praha 2 (Nové Město), Třída Vítězného února

Střed Station (Praha Střed)
Praha 1 (Nové Město), Hybernská ulice 13
This was the station from which the first train ran from Prague to Vienna in 1845.

Train information

ČSD, Tel. 24 44 41–49

Excursions

Čedok, Tel. 22 42 51–59
ČKM-SSM, Tel. 29 99 41

Restaurants

Restaurants are classed in four categories according to quality, amenity and price. The category of a restaurant is shown by a Roman figure on the menu.

Bohemian specialties: see Food and drink

Luxury category

Zlatá Praha, on top floor of Intercontinental Hotel, Praha 1, náměstí Curieových (reservation essential)
Jalta, Václavské náměstí 45 (top floor)

Restaurants with international cuisine

Alcron, Praha 1, Štěpánská 40
Ambassador, Praha 1, Václavské náměstí 5
Barrandov, Praha 5, Kříženeckého náměstí 322 (closed outside season)
Esplanade, Praha 1, Washingtonova 19
Flora, Praha 3, Vinohradská 121
Intercontinental (ground floor), Praha 1, náměstí Curieových
International, Praha 6, náměsti Družby 1
Olympik, Praha 8, Invalidovna
Oživlé dřevo, Praha 1, Strahovské nádvoří

Palace, Praha 1, Panská 12
Pelikan, Praha 1, Na Příkopě 7
Praha Expo 58, Praha 7, Letenské sady
Savarin, Praha 1, Na Příkopě 10
Vikárka, Praha 1 (Hradčany), Vikářská 6
Vysočina, Praha 1, Národní 28

Baltic Grill (Rybárna), Praha 1, Václavské náměstí 43: fish and
poultry
Fregata, Praha 2 (Vyšehrad), Ladova 3: fish
Representační dům, Praha 1, náměstí Republiky 1090: proper
diet | Speciality restaurants

Paříž, Praha 1, U Obecního domu 1 | Slovak cuisine

Činská restaurace, Praha 1, Vodičkova 19 | Chinese cuisine

Berjozka, Praha 1, Rytířska 7
Gruzia, Praha 1, Na Příkopě 29
Moskva, Praha 1, Na Příkopě 29 | Russian cuisine

Sofia, Praha 1, Václavské náměstí 33 | Bulgarian cuisine

Praha 1, Maislova 18 | Jewish cuisine (kosher)

Barrandov, Praha 5, Kříženeckého náměstí 322 (closed outside
season)
Savarin, Praha 1, Na Příkopě 10 | Garden and terrace
restaurants

Hanavský Pavilón, Praha 7, Letenské sady
Kajetánka, Praha 1 (Hradčany)
Mánes, Praha 1, Gottwaldovo nábřeží 1
Na Baště, Praha 1 (Hradčany)
Slovanský ostrov, Praha 1, Slovanský ostrov
U Lorety, Praha 1, Loretánské náměstí 8
Zlate studní, Praha 1, U zlaté studně 166 | Other restaurants

Plzenský dvůr, Praha 7, Obránců míru 59
U Bonaparta, Praha 1, Nerudova 29
U černého vola, Praha 1, Loretánské náměstí 1
U dvou koček, Praha 1, Uhelny trh 10
°U Fleků, Praha 1, Křemencova 11
U Glaubiců, Praha 1, Malostranské náměstí 5
°U Kalicha, Praha 2, Na bojišti 13
U kocoura, Praha 1, Nerudova 2
U medvidků, Praha 1, Na Perštýně 7
U Pinkasů, Praha 7, Jungmannova 15
U Schnellů, Praha 1, Tomášská 2
U Sojků, Praha 7, Obránců míru 40
U supa, Praha 1, Celetná 22
U svatého Tomáše, Praha 1, Letenská 12
U zlatého tygra, Praha 1, Husova 17 | Beer-parlours

Intercontinental, Praha 1, náměstí Curieových
Klášterní vinárna, Praha 1, Národní 8
Lobkovická vinárna, Praha 1, Vlašská 17
Lví Dvůr, Praha 1 (Hradčany), U Prasněho mostu 6
Makarská vinárna, Praha 1, Malostranské náměstí 2
Obecní dům, Praha 1, náměstí Republiky 1090
Opera-Grill, Praha 1, Divadelní 24
Slovenská vinárna, Praha 1, Františkánská zahrada | Wine-bars

U Golema, Praha 1, Maislova 8
U labutí, Praha 1, Hradčanské náměstí 11
U malířů, Praha 1, Maltézské náměstí 11
U pavouka, Praha 1, Betlémské náměstí
U zlaté stíky, Praha 1, Dlouhá 9
Vinný sklípek pana Broučka, Praha 1 (Hradčany)
U palcátu, Praha 1, Thunovská 16
U patrona, Praha 1, Dražického náměstí 4
U piaristů, Praha 1, Panská 1
U plebána, Praha 1, Betlémské náměstí 10
U Rudolfa, Praha 1, Maislova 3
U tři housliček, Praha 1, Nerudova 12
U zelené žáby, Praha 1, U radnice 8
U zlaté hrušky, Praha 1, Novy svět 3
U zlatého jelena, Praha 1, Celetná 11
°U zlaté konvice, Praha 1, Melantrichova 20

Shopping

Tuzex	The State-run Tuzex shops sell goods only for convertible foreign currency or "Tuzex crowns", which can be bought in Czechoslovak banks at the official rate of exchange. Visitors should keep all receipts for purchases in Tuzex shops. Information on duty-free export of goods purchased: Tuzex, Praha 1 (Staré Město), Rytířská 13. When buying crystal, *objets d'art*, etc., visitors should seek advice from Tuzex staff, since some articles of this kind are subject to heavy export duties. Tuzex takes care of all formalities and arranges dispatch.
Tuzex shops	Antiques: Staré Město, Rytířská 43 Glass, china, perfume, souvenirs: Staré Město, Železná 18 Perfume: Nové Město, Smečky 23 Textiles, ladies' underwear: Nové Město, Spálená 4 Ladies' and children's clothing: Praha 7, Jancovcova 2 Furs, clothing: Praha 1, Lazarská 82
Angling (fishing) gear	Praha 1, Národní třída 28 Praha 1, Vodičkova ulice 30 Praha 1, Malé náměstí 14
Antiques	See Antiques
Art (Dílo galleries)	Nové Město, Vodičkova 32 Platýz, Staré Město, Narodní 37 Karolina, Staré Město, Železná 6 Zlatá lilie, Staré Město, Malé náměstí 12 Praha 1 (Hradčany), Zlatá ulička (Golden Lane) Praha 7 (Holešovice), Obránců míru 22 Praha 4 (Nusle), Nuselská 5
Books	Kniha, Praha 1, Štepánská 42 (literature in foreign languages) Kniha, Praha 1, Vodičkova 21 (particularly illustrated books) Kniha, Praha 1 (Malá Strana), Mostecká 22 (second-hand) Kniha, Praha 1 (Staré Město), Karlova 2 (second-hand) Kniha, Praha 1 (Staré Město), Karlova 14 (graphic art, etc.) Československý spisovatel, Praha 1, Národní 9 Knihkupectví Melantrich, Praha 1, Na Příkopě 3–5 Knihkupectví U zlatého klasu, Praha 1, Na Příkopě 23

Nové Město, Spálená 4   Clothing
Praha 7, Jancovcova 2

Ustav kosmetiky, Praha 1 (Nové Město), Jungmannova 31:   Cosmetics and personal
beauty salon   services
Jeannette, Praha 1, Pařížská 7: cosmetics
Praha 1, Ve Smečkách 22: hairdresser
Praha 1, Na Příkopě 12 (Černá růže arcade): hairdresser,
cosmetics
Hygie-Zuzana, Praha 1, Václavské náměstí 66: hairdresser
Praha 1, Štěpánská 57: hairdresser
Praha 1, Václavské náměstí 28 (Alfa arcade): barber
Dům obuvi, Praha 1, Václavské náměstí 6: footwear, pedicure

Praha 1, Václavské náměstí 33   Flowers
Praha 1, Národní třída 19
Flower-stalls in the streets and outside the Central Station

Česka jizba, Praha 1, Karlova 12   Folk art
Slovenská izba, Praha 1, Václavské náměstí 40
ÚLUV, Praha 1, Národní 36
UVA, Praha 1, Na Příkopě 25

All in Praha 1:   Glass, including crystal, and
Bohemia-Moser, Na Příkopě 12 (accepts foreign currency)   china
Bohemiaglas, Parižská 2
Malé náměstí 6 (glass from Bor-Haida)
Václavské náměstí 3 (cut crystal)
Národní třída 43
Železná 18

All in Praha 1:   Jewellery
Bijoux de Bohême, Staroměstské náměstí 6
Na Příkopě 12
Václavské náměstí 53
Vodičkova 39
Národní třída 25
28. října 3
Obchodni dům Družba, Václavské náměstí 21 (garnet
jewellery)

Malá Strana, Mostecká 9   Records (Supraphon)
Staré Město, Celetná 8
Nové Město, Jungmannova 20
Nové Město, Jindřišská 19
Nové Město, Václavské náměstí 17
Nové Město, Václavské náměstí 51

Praha 1, Národní třída 38   Shooting (hunting)
Praha 1, Pařížská 5, U Huberta   equipment
Praha 1, Celetná 30
Praha 2, Vyšehrad, Ladova 7

All in Praha 1:   Souvenirs
Václavské náměstí 47, Tel. 26 56 87
Staroměstské náměstí 6, Tel. 6 05 93
Celetná 1, Tel. 6 64 03
Malé náměstí 10, Tel. 26 28 35

Spálená 4   Textiles

See Department stores

Sightseeing

City tours	City sightseeing tours are operated by: Čedok, Praha 1, Na Příkopě 18, Tel. 2 42 51 (with commentary in foreign languages)
	Pragatur, Praha 1, U Obecního domu, Tel. 6 16 51–3 (with commentary in Czech and foreign languages)
Special interest tours	"Historic Prague" (daily throughout the year) "Prague by Night" (Wed. and Fri., May to Oct.), with dinner and programme of entertainments
Special tours	For information about special tours: Tel. 54 44 44
Excursions	Čedok also organises coach trips into the country round Prague.
	See Boat trips on the Vltava

Sports

General information on sport can be obtained by telephone from the Sport-Turist travel agency, Tel. 26 33 51, 82 05 58.

A selection of sports facilities in Prague:

Football   Stadion Bohemians ČKD, Praha 10, Vršovice, SNB 2

Sightseeing by boat

Stadion Dukla, Praha 6 (Dejvice), Na Julisce 28 (army football)

SK Slavia, Praha IPS, Praha 10, Vršovice, Stadion dr. V. Vacka (football and swimming stadium)

Sparta CKD Praha, Praha 7, Letná, Obránců míru 98

State Racecourse, Chuchle	Horse-racing
Praha 4, Podoli, Podolská 74	Swimming stadium
Sportcamp TJ Slavia VŠ, Praha 5, Motol, V podháji Klamovka, Praha 5 (Košíře): covered courts	Tennis

Swimming-pools

Občanská plovárna Malá Strana, Nábřeží kpt. Jaroše	River baths on Vltava (summer only)
Slovanska plovárna Nové Město, Slovanský ostrov (opposite National Theatre; also sauna)	
Žluté lázně	
Císařska louka, Praha 5 (opposite Vyšehrad)	Open-air pools
Džbán, Praha 6, Vokovice	
Ostrov Stvanice, Praha 7, Holešovice	
Tichá Šárka, Pod Matějem, Praha 6, Dejvice	
V šáreckém údolí	
Praha 4, Podolí, Podolská 74 (also sauna and open-air pool)	Indoor pools
S.S. Slavia, Praha 10, Vršovice Stadion dr. V. Vacka (also sauna)	
Park kultury a oddechu J. Fučíka, Praha 7, U sjezdového Paláce	
Klárov, Praha 1, Nábřeží kapitána. Jaroše 3	

Taxis

Taxis can be called by telephone, hired at taxi ranks or hailed in the street.

Tel. 24 24 41	24-hour service
Tel. 6 39 98 (Mon.–Fri. 6.45 a.m.–3.30 p.m.)	Urgent calls

151

Telephone

Local calls	For a local call from a public telephone a 1 Kčs coin is required.
Trunk calls	The charge for a three-minute call within Czechoslovakia ranges between 5 and 15 Kčs. International calls are extremely expensive.
Direct dialling	Direct dialling of international calls is possible only from certain telephone offices. The Head Post Office, Jindřišská 14, Praha 1, is open 24 hours a day.
Information	To contact Prague Information dial 120; for the rest of the country dial 27 55 51
Hotels	International calls from hotels go through the exchange, involving considerable delays.
Dialling codes	See Useful Numbers at a Glance. p 156.

Theatres

Since performances are usually sold out tickets should be bought in advance (see Information – Čedok).

Divadlo ABC (ABC Theatre)
Praha 1 (Nové Město), Vodičkova 28
Comedies

Atelier Ypsilon
Praha 1 (Nové Město), Spálená 16
Music and text

Divadlo E. F. Buriana (Burian Theatre)
Praha 1 (Nové Město), Na poříčí 26
Formerly an avant-garde theatre

DISK
Praha 1 (Staré Město), Karlova 8
Young actors and actresses, classical repertoire

Laterna Magica
Praha 1 (Nové Město), Národní třída 40
A combination of music, drama, dancing, mining and film

Palác kultury (Palace of Culture)
Praha 2 (Vyšehrad)
Mixed programme

Lyra Pragensis
Praha 1 (Hradčany), Hradčanské náměstí 8
Cabaret

Music theatres
See Music

Národní divadlo (National Theatre)
Praha 1 (Nové Město), Národní třída
Opera, ballet, drama

Divadlo S. K. Neumanna (Neumann Theatre)
Praha 8 (Libeň), Rudé armády 34
A popular suburban theatre

Realistické divadlo (Realist Theatre)
Praha 5 (Smíchov), ulice S. M. Kirova 57
Socialist realism, topical plays

Reduta
Praha 1 (Nové Město), Národní třída 10
Little theatre

Činoherné klub (Drama Club)
Praha 1 (Nové Město), Ve smečkách 40

Černé divadlo (Black Theatre)
No permanent company

Divadlo Semafor (Semaphore Theatre)
Praha 1 (Nové Město), Václavské náměstí 28
Musical comedy, mime

Smetana Theatre
See Music

Divadlo Na zábradlí (Theatre at the Railings)
Praha 1 (Staré Město), Anenské náměstí 5
Mime

Tylovo divadlo (Tyl Theatre)
Praha 1 (Staré Město), Železná ulice 11
Plays, Mozart operas

Divadlo na Vinohradech (Vinohrady Theatre)
Praha 2 (Vinohrady), náměstí Míru 7
Classical and contemporary plays

Kabarett u Fleků   Cabaret
Praha 1 (Nové Město), Křemencova 11

Divadlo Rokoko (Rococo Theatre)
Praha 1 (Nové Město), Václavské náměstí 38

Variété Praga
Praha 1 (Nové Město), Vodičkova 30

Albatros   Children's and young
Praha 1 (Staré Město), Na Perštýně 1   people's theatres

Loutka Puppet Theatre
Praha 2 (Nové Město), náměstí Maxima Gorkého 28

Říše loutek (Puppet Kingdom)
Praha 1 (Staré Město), Žatecká ulice

Slunicko
Praha 1 (Staré Město), Na Příkopě 15

153

Divadlo Spejbla a Hurvínka (Spejbl and Hurvinek)
Praha 2 (Vinohrady), Římská 45

Divadlo Jiřího Wolkera (Jiří Wolker Theatre)
Praha 1 (Staré Město), Dlouhá třída 39

Time

Czechoslovakia observes Central European Time, one hour ahead of Greenwich Mean Time, seven hours ahead of Eastern Standard Time.

From May to September Summer Time (Daylight Saving Time), one hour ahead of Central European Time, is in force.

Tipping

Although a service charge is included in bills, a tip of 5–10 per cent is never unwelcome.

Travel agencies

Čedok
See Information

ČKM–SSM
(Youth Travel Agency)
Praha 2, Žitná 12

Praha 1, Opletalova 29
(Specially for motorists)

Balnea
Praha 1, Parižská 11
(Spa treatment)

Travel documents

Passport

All visitors to Czechoslovakia must have a passport, valid for at least five months at the time of application for a visa.

Visa

All visitors must have a visa, which is valid for three months and for a single visit to Czechoslovakia not exceeding 30 days (though this period may be extended on application to the Passport and Visa Office, Praha 3, Olšanská 3, or any regional passport office). Visas are obtainable from Czechoslovakian embassies and consulates, and normally take between a week and a month to process. Two passport photographs must be enclosed with the completed visa application form. A fee (at present £10 in the United Kingdom, $12 in the United States) is charged.

It is convenient to apply for a visa through Čedok (not charge for visitors travelling on one of their inclusive tours, a small service charge for others).
The visa is valid only if the requirement as to obligatory currency exchange (see Currency) has been satisfied.

Not required.   Vaccination certificate

Youth hostels

Juniorhotel (mainly for students under 30), Praha 2, Žitná 12
Information from ČKM–SSM Youth Travel Agency (see Travel agencies)

Useful Telephone Numbers

Emergencies	
General	155
Fire	150
Police	158
Ambulance	333
Breakdown assistance	22 49 06
Dental emergency service	26 13 74
Information	
General information on Prague	54 44 44
Bus services	22 14 45
Cinema programmes	145
City tours	22 42 51
Theatres and concerts (afternoon)	144
Tickets (admission)	24 90 57, 24 87 83
Time	112
Train services	24 44 41
Weather forecast	116
Embassies	
United Kingdom	53 33 47–9, 53 33 40, 53 33 70
United States	53 66 41–8
Canada	32 69 41
Airlines	
Czechoslovak Air Lines	26 96 03
British Airways	24 08 47–8
Lufthansa	31 75 51
Lost property	6 01 44
Taxis	24 24 41
Telephone	
Information, Prague	120
Information, ČSSR	121
Dialling codes	
From the United Kingdom	010 42 2
From the United States or Canada	011 42 2
To the United Kingdom	00 44
To the United States or Canada	001
Telegrams	127

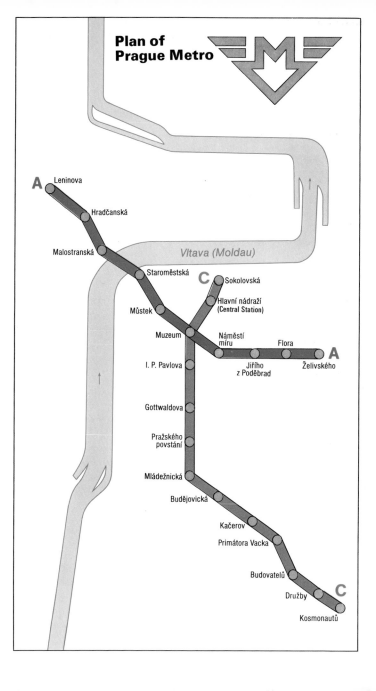

Plan of Prague Metro

A Leninova

Hradčanská

Malostranská

Vltava (Moldau)

Staroměstská

C Sokolovská

Můstek

Hlavní nádraží
(Central Station)

Muzeum

Náměstí míru

Flora

I. P. Pavlova

Jiřího z Poděbrad

Želivského **A**

Gottwaldova

Pražského povstání

Mládežnická

Budějovická

Kačerov

Primátora Vacka

Budovatelů

Družby

C

Kosmonautů

Notes

Notes